For Barb

Stories from "I

Mamai heart to

encourage yours.

Jan Jensen Carlberg

4-17-10

Stories from the Beach Chair

By Margaret T. Jensen

DEDICATION

Dedicated to the "little people" who will return to the sea, long after their "Great Grammy La La" has gone Home.

Lily and baby Luke Willis
Gracynne and baby Lund Jensen

They will come and build castles in the sand and when the tide comes in, their dream castles will wash out to the sea... They will return to build again.

SPECIAL THANKS

Thank you, Robin Perry for taking my jumbled words and putting them together. Thank you for your patience, thank you for your love and thank you for your commitment to these *Stories from the Beach Chair.*

Thank you to Carolyn Livengood for putting all my words into the computer making it possible to publish.

Thank you, Peter Vinal for a delightful afternoon of taking pictures at the beach. Your wonderful photography also tells the story.

Thank you Gordon College Publishing for turning my stories into books. Your hard work is most appreciated.

Thank you God for *always* being there for each one of us, in the sunny days at the beach, and in the darker days of our hurting. Thank you for always keeping your promises.

ENDORSEMENTS

It is an honor when noted authors write an endorsement for a book, and I deeply appreciate it.

Somehow it seems right to record messages from the hearts of my children; those loving thoughts will stay on my heart for always.

I thank every one of you,
Grammy

Thank you, Mama,

Your gifts to this family are many; God's grace is showered on us through you, your prayers, your example of obedience to God and your faithfulness en-route to your true Home. Thanks for loving us as though we have arrived- we have a long way to go!

Keep the standard high and the prayers coming. "I'll love you forever" honored to call you my Mama.

Jan Dawn

Dear Mom,

You helped us make memories and cement family ties; watch our children bond, love and argue. Local shrimp provided nourishment for the body and you encouraged our spirits to bask in God's creation. Thanks for introducing each new generation to its healing joy.

Love,
Jud

Mom,

You are the gift for all of us. Thank you for the beach house, a place where we share you and make memories for eternity. I love you and will carry on the tradition. It was so much fun to read my stories to everyone and thanks for the encouragement.

Love,
Ralph

Another wonderful summer of heaven together with family. Thank you for all you are, your faith, your hope, your never ending joy. These are the greatest gifts to us.

Love,
Chris

Gram,

Thank you! Thank you! We love you and love coming to be with you. Thanks for making it possible.

Love,
Heather

Thank you, Grammy for another great vacation on our island, family, fun, sun, sand and long dinners. The perfect break.

We love you,
Matt

Grammy Grubby,

It feels like we've been here forever! I love this place, the verandas, the rocking chairs, the ocean breeze blowing through the old house - cool, really cool!

I love it and I love you.

No. 1 Grandson,
Chad

Dearest Grammy,

Just want to thank you for always putting forth such an effort to have us all together every summer. I pray the tradition will never end.

I love you very much,
Lundy (Eric)

Grandma,

Thank you for all the love and advice you have given us over the years. We love and appreciate you.

Love,
Clover

Gram,

It has been wonderful to be with all my cousins and means more to us than we could ever say. We love you very, very much.

Kathryn Elise & Ernie

Grammy,

I just can't thank you enough for all you do to keep the grandkids happy. You are truly the greatest Grammy.

I love you so much,
Sarah

Thanks so much for the tender love. I feel very fortunate for all the time spent together.

Love,
Tommy

Grammy,

I love you all so much. I can't wait to come home to the beach. My job is not done yet.

With love from Baghdad,
Shawn

CONTENTS

INTRODUCTION

Stories From the Beach Chair

The beach house looked lonely, standing guard over the rolling ocean and deserted shore. With my tote bag weighted down with books, pen, and yellow legal pads I adjusted my beach chair and wiggled my toes in the cool sand. When the tourists go home, the "old timers" come with their chairs to reclaim the ocean. Across the wide expanse of beautiful Wrightsville Beach, North Carolina, few stragglers were seen playing tag with the surf. It was quiet except for the cry of seagulls and pounding surf. The happy voices of children building castles in the sand belonged to summer. Now and then a cool breeze reminded me that winter was not far behind. With an unopened book in my lap I looked out over the white caps and relived the time when the beach house was the gathering place for the family---just a few months ago. Now the beach house was closed until next year. The ocean had called us all together, just as Harold said 25 years ago. This was the right thing to do. Just like that! "There have been some difficult changes in the past and I don't want to leave beautiful Greensboro---my home, church, work, friends---and my sister. Why do I have to give up everything just because he thinks it is the Lord's will? God didn't talk to me about it!" I looked out over the endless roll of the sea and remembered my bitter words---twenty-five years ago. Somehow I could almost see my sister's beautiful face and hear her gentle answer, "trust God in Harold!" It turned out to be the best move we ever made. So it came to pass that we came with fear and trembling and moved into two small houses a block apart.

Ralph, our son, began his furniture business in a garage behind the small blue house on Oakcrest Drive. Now he has the Master's Touch in Dutch Square Industrial Park. Christine, his wife, came with baby Sarah, Shawn, and Eric. In the meantime Harold had painted the interior of both houses with pastel colors to welcome the 'unhappy campers". Sarah's room was in yellow and white. Eric complained, "I want my crib." "Eric, baby Sarah needs your crib, and you are a big boy," I tried to reason with him. "I don't want to be a big boy! I want my crib." "Let's take a nap on the big boy bed; you hold your teddy bear and I'll hold you." I coaxed.

When I don't know what to do I usually either go to the bathroom, take a nap, or put on the coffee pot. This was a good time for a nap. Eric wanted his crib, and I wanted my house in Greensboro. After the nap Eric said, "Sarah can have my crib. I'm a big boy now.' That's when I put on the coffeepot---twenty-five years ago! Now Harold was Home! From his "view from the top" I'm sure he could see his children coming to the sea. Why did it all seem like yesterday? The years run together.

Our daughter, Janice, is married to Judson Carlberg, president of Gordon College. She called to say they were arriving from Boston on Friday. Their daughter, Heather, is married to Matt; they are both in medical school and were coming from Philadelphia. My book stayed in my lap unopened. I was just remembering a long ago time when the three year old Heather stood, feet apart, hands on her hips, looking out to sea. "Grammy, did God make everything?" "Oh, yes, He did!" "Did he make the ocean?" "Yes," I answered. "Why did He have to make it so big?" Now she and Matt would be surfing in those big waves. "Way to go, Grammy, a beach house for two weeks---cool, Grammy, cool! Your number one grandson is on his way!" That was Chad, Heather's brother, en route from California. Eric, with his wife Clover, were coming from Tennessee, so Ralph and Chrissy would have their family together also. Beach towels, folding chairs, surf boards, and umbrellas filled the cars as they come from all directions. Airport schedules were posted on the refrigerator.

When Jan arrived Chrissy joined her to make up beds and stock the refrigerator. I turned my car to Sam's Wholesale and filled it with cases of toilet tissue, paper plates, and napkins---taking no chances. The beach house was silent, closed for the winter, but I could hear the sounds of a family coming home. "Oh Mom, I love this old house---high ceilings and open windows that allow sea breezes to blow day and night," said Ralph. Old books lined the shelf, while rocking chairs waited on the porch. A hammock swayed in the wind. "Look, Jan, big kettles for shrimp and corn.--and frying pans for the fish our men will catch," added Chris. "Mom, look, there is a small room and bath on the first floor---no extra steps to climb---just made for you," observed Ralph. I chuckled to myself, knowing my own plans were to head for my own bed---before the after dinner nap. The girls insisted, 'No cooking, Mom---we'll do it!" I knew that if I stayed I'd be the first one up in the morning, and the "no cooking" rule would blow away---bacon, eggs, and pancakes danced in my head. I was recalling, "Oh, Mom, aren't you spending the night?" Jan asked, but I answered "I need to feed Scarlet---and I'll come back in the morning. It's only ten minutes away." (What I really meant was that when you get older there is no comfort like your own bed---they could put up with sand blowing in the bed.) When I got in my car I laughed out loud. I had slipped out of that in a hurry, and now my Doberman and I would enjoy a quiet evening with a good book. I told her all about it and she agreed. Someone said it is healthy to talk to your dog. We are staying healthy!

Somehow I managed to load the car with a honey-baked ham, potato salad, baked beans, and a chocolate cake for Eric. On Sunday the usual beef roast found its way to the beach---and a lemon pie for Jud. Then I gracefully slipped away "to take care of the dog". Scarlet was grinning---yes, she was! "We like our early morning coffee, don't we?" I reached for my book and a cup of tea. Scarlet stretched out over my feet with her head in my lap. There's something comforting about routine. The older I get, the more I enjoy the re-runs of the past.

I didn't get any writing done that day, and my book stayed shut, so I folded my beach chair, slipped into my sandals, and walked slowly through the sea grasses. I looked up at the beach house that had withstood the hurricanes and looked like a fortress against the wind and sea. "How can a house withstand the storm, but our homes are blown away, leaving scattered debris of broken hearts and broken dreams that wash out to sea on currents of man's philosophy?" Looking back over the years I recalled the celebrations of marriages that held fifty, sixty years of commitment to God and each other---great grandparents, grandparents, aunts, uncles, parents. How did they stand? The storms came---storms of the Great Depression, epidemics, black clouds of war; still the families stood- in gain or loss, joy or sorrow. Reminds me of the words of an old hymn,
"They had an anchor that kept the soul
Steadfast and sure while the billows roll."

I looked up at the beach house. The wind was blowing sand across the porches, and the rockers were turned to the wall---a safe harbor. "Oh God," I prayed, "for all our young people who laughed, swam, surfed, and dipped their shrimp in cocktail sauce---even those who slid the ears of corn over the butter dish (Eric!) or ate the frosting (Chad!) or forgot the ice for the ice cream freezer (Shawn!)---for those who played games, retold family stories in renditions I didn't recognize--- oh God, may their homes stand against the winds of a culture that beats against the eternal values that keep us strong."

"Take your place, children," I called out to the wind, "know the Truth that sets you free." The gathering clouds looked dark and threatening; the wind swept sand in my face and the pounding surf and seagulls were behind me as I hurried to the car before the thunder rolled. With a backward glance I knew I would return to write stories from the beach chair.

one

Wrightsville Beach

I eased my car out of the driveway and headed to the beach house---only ten minutes away, if the draw bridge wasn't up. It was! While I waited in the line of traffic I remembered another day more than twenty-five years ago, when I walked the isolated shoreline in the early morning. I could almost feel the wind in my face and the salt spray washing my tears of bitterness about leaving my lovely home in Greensboro to move to Wilmington, North Carolina.

For years we had come to the beautiful Wrightsville Beach, but returned home to Greensboro, family and friends. Now we were coming to Wilmington to begin all over again. I was sixty-two and I didn't like change. "Trust God!" my sister Doris said. "Praise God," Lena shouted. "In everything give thanks," I seemed to hear from my Norwegian mama. By faith, that is what I did. How could I have known that the best years of my life were just ahead!

I watched the sailboats pass while the bridge was going down. Moving slowly with the traffic I turned toward the beach house and managed to squeeze into the limited parking space. "Chad will back out for me," I thought to myself." With my tote bag filled with books, paper, and pen I followed the path, lined with wild flowers and plants, up the steps to a screened-in porch with a long picnic table set for supper---a tradition of shrimp, corn-on-the-cob, and homemade ice cream. Since I had strict orders to stay out of the kitchen I humbly took my place in a rocking chair on the porch to read a book. "Huh! they'll find out they can't handle the kitchen without me," I muttered to myself. I found out! *They could!* When I peeked, Jud was stirring the shrimp to a delicate pink while Chrissy piled the corn on a plate. Jan took a swipe at the salad and Ralph plugged in the ice cream freezer. In the meantime the "beachers" were washing off sand and reaching for dry shorts and tops.

I returned to my book, thinking that I could get used to this turn of events, and made mental plans for next year. "Here comes Uncle Peter!" Katie Elise ran to meet Peter Stam, who was married to my youngest sister, Jeanelle, until God took our angel Home. "Grammy, Uncle Peter belongs to our family, so don't let anyone take him away from us," said Katie Elise. When political, theological, and social issues arise, the young people in our family listen to the wisdom of Peter's years of experience---as a missionary in Africa and as a student of great books and the Bible. Steps of great men still draw the young to follow.

"Well, Margaret, I see you are not in the kitchen!" he grinned. "Strict orders---and I think I'm getting used to it." Katie Elise rang the bell that brought us to the table, where we joined hands while Ralph asked the blessing. Ten pounds of shrimp made its way around the table, followed by corn and salad. While we peeled our own shrimp, the cocktail sauce and stories made the rounds. Katie Elise and I used to peel Papa's shrimp so he wouldn't get his fingers sticky; we spoiled him." Papa, their beloved grandfather, my true love, Harold, had fourteen seasons at the beach until God called him home in 1991. Sarah was the "princess" and according to her Papa, she "could do no wrong". "Oh! Oh! Grammy, Eric is doing it again---slipping his corn over the butter dish." No secrets in this family---Katie Elise sees to that! "How many years have we been coming to this beach?" asked Chad. "We came a long time before you were born Chad. Someone found a place to rent near Mercers' pier, but when your Papa realized how noisy it was he was ready to head for Florida. But someone suggested a lovely place on the sound side of Wrightsville Beach and that is where your mother and her brothers learned to water ski.

When we were offered a place on Crane Drive for $50.00 a week we kept returning there each year. We saved all year to have the extra money for that one wonderful week on Crane Drive. Harold and I enjoyed the quiet drive at night, with the windows down for cool breezes---no air conditioning in those days.

We'd leave Greensboro, NC about 4 a.m., and be in Wilmington before 9 a.m. for breakfast. A trip to the farmer's stand would help us fill up the car with fresh vegetables and fruit.

One morning at the beach, Harold and I decided to go for an early morning walk so we slipped out quietly while Jan, Dan, and Ralph were sleeping. Hand in hand we walked along the vast ocean shore, drinking in the beauty of the early morning, the sound of the sea, and the cry of seagulls. It was one of those molten moments when the soul catches up with the body---when the cares of the world are left behind and the wonder of it all fills up the empty places. We were all alone at that moment; the sun, the sky, the ocean belonged to us. Harold turned and said, "Oh,oh. we are not alone---three musketeers are following." Jan, always the instigator, had opened her brown eyes and saw us slip out for a walk, so she prodded the boys awake to play 'Follow the Leader'.

For a moment there was silence. Then Chad spoke up, "Grammy, looks like we are still doing it---following Papa's footprints in the sand---fifty years later." "Do you suppose he's watching?" "I wouldn't be surprised." I said.

It was time for ice cream. I rose to serve when Jan's look said "sit still Mom". Uncle Peter nudged me and chuckled. Cool breezes blew around the porches, and we shivered with our bowls of ice cream. For a moment I hesitated---then I saw a mug of coffee coming my way. "You didn't think we would forget coffee," exclaimed Jan. (I wasn't sure.)

"Mom, didn't an elderly lady offer the Crane Drive house to Papa?" asked Jan. "Yes, she wanted us to have it and offered it for $50.00 a month. I really think she saw how much we enjoyed it and tried to make a way for us to buy it. At that time it seemed impossible, and we allowed that blessing to slip away. We lived to regret that lack of vision---and to appreciate the offer that had been made to us. Sometimes God has blessings to give but we don't know how to receive his surprises. 'As a man thinks, so is he.' Our thinking was limited to a concept in our day: 'Keep the preacher humble, and we will keep him poor'. "Oh, Grammy, to think we could have had that house all these years," lamented Chad. "It's true. But we can't look back; for when you do the best you can at the time, it is pointless to be eaten with regret. So, now we concentrate on the blessing we have and leave the past to God's grace and mercy," I explained. We warmed our hands around our coffee mugs---and continued eating ice cream. The evening was coming to an end. It was time to check on Scarlet, my faithful Doberman. Chad held my arm down the stairs and offered to back out my car. I hugged my number one grandson and heard, 'I love you Grammy Grubby." "I love you, too, my number one" and we each knew we meant it.

When I pulled into the driveway I heard a "welcome home" bark, and we were back to the routine---fresh water and a snack for Scarlet, and a replay of the evening. 'Believe it or not, Scarlet, they wouldn't let me in the kitchen. And the worst part---they managed without me!" Scarlet laughed! Oh yes, she did! (She ran in circles. That's what she does when there is something funny going on.) I put on my robe and slippers and brushed my hair, ready for bed. Then I curled up in Harold's leather chair to read for an hour. Scarlet stood beside me, looking intently into my face with dog devotion; then she settled down with her head in my lap.

I picked up a new book, <u>Plain Talk and Common Sense</u>, by Kenneth Hamblin.

You can give a man a house, but not a home. Homes are the stuff of dreams and youthful ambitions. They are the illusions of optimistic young people aspiring---sometimes against odds---to a bright future.

Softly, like a gentle breeze, came the memories of a long ago time when a ten year old girl sat---with a bowl of oatmeal and whole wheat bread with sugar---and heard stories of faith, listened to the strumming of a guitar, and dared to dream.

Tonight my children will sleep with the music of the sea and dream their dreams. "Come Scarlet, time for bed." I called. She curled up with her blanket in the laundry room. I locked the doors, turned out the lights, and hugged my down pillow. "Thank you, Lord, for my own bed."

I have miles to go---but tonight I sleep.

two

The Swim Suit

After my morning coffee I decided to meet the family at the beach house. I packed my tote bag with books, pen, and paper, and then scurried for my bathing suit and extra towels. When the phone rang I knew it was Jan. It was! "Mom, aren't you coming?" "I can't find my bathing suit," I said. "Good! You were supposed to give those ten year old suits to Goodwill. Maybe this time you did it. Just stop at Redix and get a new one---badly needed, I might add," was her instruction. Reluctantly I pulled into the parking lot where the beach store had 'Big Sale' signs. The sale didn't work for me, since the only suit that looked like the one I couldn't find was $98.00! I choked down the guilt and bought the suit. After all, I couldn't keep the family waiting for me.

"I see that you finally bought a new suit, Mother. But what is that string in the back?" asked Jan. "The shoulder straps kept slipping off my shoulders, so I just tied the back straps together with this string. To think this suit cost $98.00. I'll never get over that!" I tried to explain that I didn't want straps sliding off my shoulders when my two grandsons, Chad and Shawn, helped me through the surf to swim in calmer waters. It's wasn't that I had anything extraordinary to reveal, but I'm of the opinion that mystery and intrigue make life interesting. The bikini-clad beauties seem convinced that "less is better". When I watch the old movies I admire the actors who can make displaying an ankle look provocative. Imagination is a great gift.

One day, sitting around the table with friends of long standing (not supposed to say *old* friends) we laughed about how modest we were in our day---never saw a navel until we married. Sometimes I'm glad Harold isn't around to hear all about this new kind of sex. We never thought the old sex needed improvement and believed that marriage was a good discovery channel for both navels and sex. Most men, even those married over fifty years, will lament, "I'll never understand women!" That's just how it's supposed to be---mystery and intrigue!

Now what's this business about rings in the navel? I usually discuss these issues with Scarlet, since there is so much sex on television; I surely don't want to add to the new enlightenment. Scarlet understands and does not report these conversations to the media. When I was in Greece and Turkey on a Gordon College tour we stopped to watch people take pictures of huge stone called the "navel of the world". I looked up navel: "The depression on the abdomen where the umbilical cord was attached; a central part or points." Not so long ago I recalled how my one year old toddler would pull up a shirt and happily point to the "belly button". It was cute then; I fail to see the cuteness in grown adolescents hiking up a shirt to reveal a ring in a belly button. When the little ones were in the tub I used to get a cotton swab to keep the belly button clean.

One day in my early morning coffee time I was reading about Job. God talked about a behemoth (a colossal animal like an elephant)---that has his strength in his loins and his force in the navel of his belly; he's not afraid of anything. (Job 40:16) I turned to Proverbs and read that trusting the Lord, not always depending on our own understanding, acknowledging

God's authority, guidance, and wisdom, and making a choice to depart from evil---all this is health to our navel. (Proverbs 3:8) Since navel is the central point or part---that very life of the mother flowing to the child through the umbilical cord---that part of God's creation seems sacred to me. It seems great wisdom to have health at the center of life. Maybe I am getting too old for this world, but somehow I see life in its beauty and simplicity, following Biblical guidelines. It takes just as much effort to make wrong choices as it does to make good choices---but the consequences are different.

Marriage is a good "discovery channel" for physical, mental, emotional, and spiritual discoveries. In more than fifty years of marriage we knew what "is---is" and "isn't---isn't", that good sex comes with a life committed to a loving, giving, thankful heart. That discovery channel called marriage has its peaks and valleys, its passion and calm, its storms and quiet streams. It meant holding my hand when I went to radiation treatment; it was saying I was 'so cute" in a maternity dress and flat shoes; it was a cup of tea when I couldn't eat; it was a shoulder to cry on and an arm to sleep in. When the "all clear" was sounded we turned on the music and danced. When the curtain came down on the last act together I cradled Harold's head in my arms. "I love you; see you in the morning."

The day ended after a good swim. The string held the straps of my $98.00 suit. I found my ten year old suits. They were in a box marked "*Winter* Clothes---Goodwill"!

three

Ralph, the Chef

For the past few days the weather had settled over the beach with blustery winds and cold rain. No one complained because it seemed like a good time to relax after the stress of school, work, and travel. When I came to see how the 'beachers" were faring I found Chad wrapped in a blanket on the porch, Heather and Matt curled up in the hammock, and Chris and Jan devouring the new books by Jan Karon and John Grisham, with an invisible sign: "Do not disturb". I wasn't about to climb the stairs to see what the others were doing so I did the sensible thing---I curled up in my corner room and took a nap. It came to pass that the rain stopped and the sun broke out in golden splendor. Then came Ralph's announcement that he would grill his famous mini-steaks for supper. When an invitation came to play golf, he took off with Eric. For the moment steaks were not on his mind---golf was!

Darkness came slipping in over the ocean, and I was about to decide that I had nibbled enough pretzels. It was time to go feed Scarlet and whip up a grilled cheese for me. (I could have told them it was a mistake to keep me out of the kitchen.) Jud returned from fishing and took Jan to Olympia for a seafood dinner. Chris found a corner---and a book. She was not about to let Ralph off the hook. Where was Ralph? Probably looking for golf balls in the dark. Just as I was leaving, "his royal highness" and Eric returned, surrounded by a wall of silence. Not missing a beat, Ralph grilled the steaks and placed them in special buns---and the feast was ready. By 10 p.m. everyone was hungry, so the "chef" came out a winner. When I returned in the morning I heard about the stories that were told into the early morning hours. "Most of them were about you, Grammy," one grandchild confessed. No wonder everyone was asleep!

I found my pen and paper and headed for the beach chair, definitely staying out of the kitchen. With my coffee cup in hand I remembered the Blue Datsun. "When you die Grammy, can I have the Blue Datsun?" asked Katie Elise. To five year old Katie Elise, the Blue Datsun was the golden chariot that carried sand buckets, big towels, and excited young'uns to the beach. "The way it looks right now, Katie Elise, the Blue Datsun will die before I do, but if she lives, you certainly can have her." Katie Elise was happy. The Blue Datsun would remain in the family forever. For some reason the Blue Datsun was a "her"---a part of the family. We talked to her, pleaded with her, screamed at her---even cried over her. We sympathized with her as she aged and became increasingly bent, broken, and bruised.

The Blue Datsun hadn't always looked like that. At one time she was shining and new. One look at her and I knew I had a friend who could face the challenges of the roads of life with me. The students at Greensboro College, where I was the college nurse, admired my excellent choice, and she was the envy of the campus. Everything else in the parking lot paled beside her shining blue armor.

One day our elder son Dan took her on a trip to the North, and my Dixie Datsun collided with a Yankee Ford. She hadn't known the war was over, and she came limping home, wounded and depressed. Her battle scars healed eventually, though, and once again she gamely hit the road.

One Christmas Eve Ralph and his friend Billy were crossing an icy bridge on their way home for our special Christmas Eve dinner. The brave little Datsun was hit by an oncoming car. Apparently the driver was under the influence of the deadly enemy, drugs. The Datsun smashed into the railing, but it held fast and the boys were kept from going into the frigid river below. The occupants of the other car also were spared, and Ralph and Billy shared their faith with them while waiting for the police to come. Our Christmas Eve dinner was a little late that night, but our hearts were filled with gratitude that all the lives had been spared.

The Blue Datsun proudly wore the "purple heart" awarded her for bravery and for injury in action, but the scars were beginning to show. Her rusted-out trunk held a board across the holes, and sand buckets and inner tubes (used as ocean liners) found a special place there. The plastic seats were held together with dark blue tape, and wet bathing suits, sticky fingers, and gum wrappers found a happy home there. Her air conditioning worked only in the winter, so in the summer all the windows would be open and the wind would blow on the children while they sang:

Sea gull, sea gull,
Up in the sky,
We can see you flying so high.
Please, oh please, don't go away---
We'll come back another day

When we reached home we would just sweep the sand out and I would put a clean towel over the front seat.

The time came when the Blue Datsun began to run down, and one day she came to a dead stop. Earlier that day she had faithfully taken me to the hospital for the 3-11 p.m, shift. My starched uniform had a clean place, and an extra hair net let the wind blow on me as I drove. During my shift the Blue Datsun stood forlornly in an obscure parking place, waiting, but at 11 p.m. she perked up, and we chugged home together. Then she died! Right there in her own familiar place. Her days of being mended and patched were over---her heart had stopped beating. That's when we hung our heads and cried over her. And then we buried her. Yet the memories live on, and the stories will keep her in the family always.

Katie Elise remembers the stories and someday she will probably write them in a book. "When I grow up, I'll be a nurse like Grammy," she has said. "When I'm too old to do anything else, I'll write books, too." We can count on it!

Later we went to the beach in a 1984 Oldsmobile, but the trunk was covered with plastic and the seats were covered with plastic and towels---no wet bathing suits on the plush seats. Gum wrappers went in containers, and Papa's 'wash your hands" kept sticky fingers off windows. The air conditioner worked, and the tape recorder played songs by Sandi Patti. And the car windows stayed up. Katie Elise sat with her beach towel. Wistfully she mourned for the old days---the days of sandy buckets, dripping inner tubes, and open windows with sand and wind in the air. Finally Katie Elise found her voice and said, "I'll never forget the Blue Datsun, Grammy. Remember the funny noises she made when we went down Oleander Drive? Everybody looked at us because it sounded like---oh, I guess I better not say what it sounded like. Anyhow, I miss her." We laughed together!

But there was another day I didn't laugh---a day when the old Blue Datsun was still running. I had been invited to the Country Club for lunch. The Blue Datsun chugged along, funny noises and all. At one point she stalled in the Oleander Drive traffic. "I'll park this old relic far away so no one will see it," I thought to myself. I found a remote corner for the Blue Datsun and joined my friends for lunch, the car forgotten. When it was time to leave, the hostess made the remark that she had to park her new Cadillac some distance away because of the limited parking space. "So did I," I told her. We walked together, and I wondered when she would get to her car. I didn't wonder long. When we reached my Blue Datsun, there was the shining new Cadillac, perched right beside it! I wanted to die! It didn't help a bit when I saw the absolute pity in her eyes!

From somewhere in the past I heard my Norwegian Mama say, "Pride is a terrible thing, Margaret. Wear you high button shoes with a thankful heart." (Those high button shoes keep coming out of the barrel of life.) "Ja, ja, Margaret, it is not so important what you have on the feet, but it is important where the feet go." "Mama was right, of course, but you're right too, Katie Elise.

We'll always remember the Blue Datsun."

PS: I think flounder is on the menu tonight---but then how would I know when I'm kept out of the kitchen? Jan and Chris are laughing, rattling pots and pans, so I'll curl up in my little room and take a nap.

four

The Sand Dunes

The weatherman said 95?, but I decided to leave my air conditioned office, pack my beach chair into the car trunk, and head to the south part of the beach where the Coast Guard is stationed. Since it had been several years since I had been there I was surprised to be greeted with meters---twenty-five cents for fifteen minutes. I dug around for quarters and found a pocketful of loose change and rolled up one dollar bills, but only three quarters. So much for my morning at the beach.

With my tote bag in hand I walked up to the small pavilion and sat down to enjoy the breeze from the ocean blowing through the sea grasses. In the distance a rocky island seemed to rise out of the sea while boats made waves. Along the shore the sand dunes with sea grasses rolled along the endless expanse of white sand. At the far end a fisherman and his young sons were throwing in their hooks. Scattered beach chairs held parents and children; since this was a "no swimming' area, the young jumped in the shallow edge while parents watched carefully. I remember when the wind would make a hollow place in the sand, and with a foot of water it was just enough for the young to jump in their "swimming pool". One lone seagull seemed to be crying for a mate---no one wants to be alone.

The wind blew through the sheltered building, and I took out pen and paper to write about a long ago time when I played hide and seek with the grandchildren. While they hid in the tall grasses I roared like a lion and, we tumbled and laughed in the sand.

The ocean looked inviting, so I put my pen down and decided to get my feet wet at the water's edge. It was then I realized how deceptively cool the white sand appears; now and then I stopped to get a deep breath until I put my feet into the refreshing water. In yesteryears I played hide and seek; today the tall lean grandsons hold my hand as we go through the surf. With only ten minutes left on the meter I realized how precious time is---meters clicking away while I drink in the beauty around me. When I returned to the shelter my tote bag had been emptied, my manuscript was blowing in the wind, and the iced Coke and change purse were gone. At first I thought the wind had blown the contents; then I knew it was a deliberate act. For fifty years I had come to this beautiful beach and left bag, keys, wallets beside a beach chair filled with soggy towels, to swim or walk the sandy shore. I was angry that our culture had changed the calm, safety, and security of a safe place to a place of fear and mistrust. What will it be like when the grandchildren bring their little ones to build castles in the sand or to play hide and seek in the sea grasses?

For me it was only the loss of a change purse and an iced Coke on a hot day, but it left me feeling vulnerable to probing eyes reading what I had written and rummaging through personal items. (I'm thankful I had my wallet in the car trunk!) Tomorrow I'll bring my beach chair to the safety of the beach house, where no meters tick away fifteen minutes for twenty-five cents. I will write where the sand meets the surf and the seagulls cry for their mates.

On my way home I stopped at Hardee's for a peach shake and hamburger and watched an older attendant rush through orders and manage a pleasant smile to the long line of customers. "What a good job you are doing!" I laughed as I gave my order. "I think I ought to help you." "Oh, if people will just be patient, I'll get it done," she smiled. 'Yes, you will---and thank you!" I wondered if whoever stole my change purse would be willing to work in a fast food place! "Help Wanted" signs seemed to be everywhere. Few seem willing to work, while the young people I know work two jobs and go to school. Our strange culture seems to punish the successful people and reward the "victim mentality". While I stood in the long line at Hardee's I saw that there was enough work for three young people willing to begin at minimum wage, then move up to bigger rewards. Many successful people today began by sweeping floors; they shouldn't be punished for climbing the ladder of hard work.

One day I left my purse in the grocery cart in the parking lot of Harris Teeter, and it wasn't until I unloaded the groceries that I realized my purse was gone. I had just gone to the bank and had two hundred dollars in cash, since I was flying out of town in the morning. With a cry of "Help, Lord!" I went back to the store; there one of the clerks was waving my purse. Nothing had been taken! I asked who brought my bag in, and a young man was paged. When I thanked him he just grinned, "My Momma brought me up right, ma'am." Sipping my peach shake I wondered about the mommas and the papas who are bringing the younguns' up right.

I was the make-believe lion roaring around the sand dunes in a long ago time. Today I realized how Satan, like a roaring lion, seeks to devour, kill, or destroy. It is a reminder for us to put on the armor of God to resist the enemy (Ephesians 6). I pulled into the driveway, washed my sandy feet, and then jumped into the shower. The day came to a close when I curled up in Harold's chair. Scarlet looked at me, then settled with her head on my lap. Her world was in order, and she brought much comfort to me. But she was not my security. My safe place is hid with Christ in God.

He hideth my soul
In the cleft of the Rock
And covers me there with his hand.

five

Seating for One

My car eased south among the Sunday morning traffic on College Road, then I turned at Monkey Junction on Piner Road to Myrtle Grove Presbyterian Church. Someone used to have a small zoo of monkeys on that corner; the name stuck long after the monkeys were gone.

In that long ago day a small white church called a new pastor, Horace Hilton, who left his large church to ease gently into retirement. It didn't turn out that way because the little white church on the side of the road started "bustin' out all over' until there was standing room only---outside! The young people came with sandaled feet, long hair, and empty souls and the gentle pastor reached into a diverse community with Biblical preaching from a loving heart. Love stretched out the walls of the little white church until it turned into a beautiful Williamsburg edifice, steeple rising to the sky.

It was Easter morning when we walked from the old white church to the new church down the road. Bill Hill, one of the elders, carried the cross beside the pastor, Horace Hilton. I carried Sarah, wearing a frilly bonnet, followed by Ralph and Chris holding Shawn and Eric. The congregation marched together singing "This is the day the Lord has made". The robed choir took their places while the orchestra tuned up; Joanne made the organ roll like we were in a great cathedral. "He lives, He lives, Christ Jesus lives today" rolled out across the open fields.

Many years later I found myself seated in the aisle seat-- alone. I looked up at the cross that had been carried that Easter morning, the cross that remained unchanged in spite of the winds of changing culture. The message of God's love is unchanging. Above the cross was the dove that Ralph carved.

For a few moments I went back in time to when Harold sat in the aisle seat; then Sarah squeezed in beside her Papa, followed by Ralph, Chris, Shawn, Eric, and Katie Elise. When we saw Steve, our nephew, coming with his family, we made room for him and Beverly, Benjamin, and Paul. "Aunt Margaret, you won't believe this family." 'Try me!" Steve chuckled out loud. "All four of us were in the bathroom. Beverly was hidden in the shower, I was shaving, and the boys were aiming in a general direction when two year old Paul said, "Too many in this bathroom---would one please leave?" We laughed all the way to church." Somehow it all seems like yesterday when we filled up a row of tow heads behind the Satterfields and their three children.

Today they sat alone! Their only son, Reid, and his wife, April, left for Africa as missionaries. Diane cried, and I cried with her. Now Harold is Home!

Ralph sits in the aisle seat with Chris beside him, and I try to keep Katie Elise from slipping in between them. Sitting close to your mate and holding hands on a Sunday morning reduces the stress level the past week drags to church. The cares of the world need to be locked in the trunk of the car. Holding a hymn book together and singing "A mighty fortress is our God, a bulwark never failing" makes the world go away for a moment of time. Yesterday---a row full of blonde heads. Today I sit alone. I see the lights of a city gleam through the rain and the mist, I could feel that lonesome feeling come over me, and I knew I missed Harold, missed the family. But it was more---I missed the memories that old hymns bring back, words and music like anchors of the soul. "When days are weary and long nights dreary," there comes a stirring from deep within: *"My faith looks up to thee, thou lamb of Calvary"*. Then the focus turns upward and I know *"It is well with my soul"*. Familiar words from old hymns renew faith for today. When the storms of life come crashing against my soul I can almost hear the choir in my Norwegian father's church in Chicago singing *"Wonderful grace of Jesus, deeper than the mighty rolling seas"*. Sometimes in the night when I am praying over a wandering sheep I can go back to sleep singing *"Be still my soul, the Lord is on thy side"*.

One day I was a speaker at a retreat for one thousand Hispanic women. After an exuberant time of singing the leader said, "I would like to hear a testimony from you---not your words, but a song that has blessed you in the past." From the back of the room a quivery voice sounded *"What a friend we have in Jesus'"* the women joined in harmony. Other voices followed with *"On a hill far away, stood an old rugged cross"*, *"Jesus loves me"*, and *"Great is thy faithfulness"*. A spontaneous hymn sing melted the women together. Needless to say it was easy to speak when God, by his spirit, prepared the hearts of his people.

When I was asked to speak in a church on the west coast I was surprised to see the changes five years had brought. When I had visited earlier the piano, organ, orchestra, and choir joined to praise God. That day there was no choir, no organ or piano---only a music team, keyboard, drums, and various instruments. Not only did this historic church have many young people, but also a large congregation of older people who lived within walking distance of their church. At the close of my message I sang an old hymn, *"At the cross, at the cross, when I first say the light, and the burden of my heart rolled away"*. Suddenly someone slipped out of the pew to the piano and picked up the key. No one wanted to stop. With tears in their eyes they sang *"Oh the blood of Jesus that cleanses white as snow"*. The old hymns seemed to wash away the debris of a broken world and its discordant sound. Someone added, "They took our memories away when they took our songs; so many new choruses that we can't remember, but the old hymns are a part of us. Thanks for the memory." It takes great wisdom to blend the cultures without losing the message.

If classical music is good for the newborn child, perhaps classical hymns might be good for the newborn souls of our day.

Since my travels bring me into many denominations I am delighted to see many young people in our services; I also see a vast source of untapped power--the older generation. These are the faithful ones who mortgaged their homes to build churches and schools; who sent their children to the mission field, prayed over the erring ones, lifted the fallen; and when shepherds came and then left, these faithful ones remained to gather the sheep and keep them in the fold. They must not be forgotten! When I look into their faces I see the keepers of the soul of America, reaching into each generation with arms of love. These keepers of the soul have a prayer in common: "Even when I am old and gray do not forsake me, oh God, until I have shown your power to the next generation". (Psalm71) The service came to a close. A young girl held her brother's hand to go to the altar to pray with an elder. I wondered what she was asking. A daddy to come home? A mommy to stop crying? She knew where to go.

I remembered a long ago time when young Katie Elise, with a ribbon tied to her ponytail, walked to the altar to pray. Later, I asked the reason. "I went to pray for my Uncle Dan. Jesus said, 'Ask.'" A child will ask.

six

The One Dresser Drawer

Ralph and Chris helped Katie Elise Jensen, the youngest grandchild, pack her belongings in a van---a computer, small refrigerator, etc.-she was off to college. I told her, "When I went to school, Katie Elise, I had one box on my lap, and while the street car rumbled along Diversey Avenue in Chicago I wondered how I would ever fill three drawers in my small dresser." "Oh, no, Grammy---now I feel bad to need a van!" she exclaimed. "We are in a different culture now, and some items are a part of education---tools for learning. You will learn from your experiences like I learned from mine; remember, it is not what's in your closet, but what you store in your heart." Then they were off, heading into the Blue Ridge Mountains of North Carolina to Montreat College.

I reached for my pen and paper and went back into another day. My sister, Grace and Doris, shared a small room with me when we were in school in Chicago. It had a small dresser with three drawers and a mini-closet; a full-sized bed was pushed up against a wall to make room for the dresser. We slept three in a bed---Grace was by the wall, Doris the youngest was in the middle, and since I was the eldest I was guardian of the edge. We'd scratch each other's back, then yell, 'Turn!' We turned!

Mama made friends with everyone, especially the Jewish peddler who came with a bag of woolen samples. My Norwegian mama admired the wool but couldn't buy, so she offered what she had---a place to rest, a cup of coffee, or a bowl of soup---and time to talk about children, the old country, and the hopes and dreams in a new world. When the Jewish peddler had new woolen samples he brought the old to Mama and she sewed the pieces together with a red feather stitch. One was the quilt for our bedroom on the second floor cold water flat (an apartment without central heat) in Chicago. A stove in the parlor and a garbage burner (a small stove) in the kitchen kept the flat warm---but not the bedrooms. The dark woolen quilt was our protection in cold Chicago winters. A small window faced a brick wall, with a narrow gangway dividing the buildings. Papa insisted on pulling down the shade at night so no preying eyes could watch his daughters. When Papa was in his study I closed the door quietly and lifted the shade so I could see a patch of sky above the bricks. With that patch of sky I dreamed of far away places---the left-behind prairies where the wind blew over the grass---and my horse Dolly who galloped along the country road while I rode bareback holding her mane. "Dolly, I love you! I'll never forget you when I go to Chicago." I never did!

One day Mama had a surprise for us! Logan Department Store had a sale on material---ten cents a yard---so she bought several yards of soft cotton print with tiny purple violets. "Ja, I will cover the dark quilt and make curtains to match." Our tiny room was transformed into a fairy land with the covered quilt and matching curtains.

Every Saturday Mama had us scrub the floor and move the bed to get in the corners. The sheets were changed---the top sheet went on the bottom, then a fresh sheet on top; starched pillow cases covered the three pillows. The beautiful quilt was the crowning touch, with spring violets at the window to hide the brick wall. Grace, Doris, and I cleaned out our one drawer each week and marveled at the wonder of our small treasures. We had to be the richest children in the world!

Days, months flew by, and somehow the years slipped away and I was packing to leave for Norwegian American Hospital for nurses' training. I was rich beyond my wildest dreams---a new coat from Mrs. Wiberg, with brown fur trim, a new store bought dress with high heeled pumps to match, and one pair of silk stockings. At a farewell party the young people gave me a watch with a second hand. Papa, oblivious to the excitement in packing my box, sat in his study and read. Everyone helped to carefully pack the underwear and cotton stockings, my one pair of silk hose, a flannel nightgown Mama made, bathrobe and slippers, a skirt and two blouses, a sweater, and good walking shoes. There was no nickel for car fare, so I was prepared to walk the four miles on my free afternoon--- through Humbolt Park to Central Park Avenue. I gathered my Bible and Streams in the Desert devotional; I read the inscription: "Happy Birthday, Margaret---April 18, 1932---from Eleanor Holby". Grace slipped a mystery package into my box "to be opened when you get there". My box was packed! Today I would wear my first store bought dress (a gift from my nurse friend, Leona), my first pair of high heeled shoes from Marshall Fields, and the new coat with the fur collar. No one could be more blessed! Papa said "goodbye" and went back to his books. Grace held baby Jeanelle, while Gordon, Doris, and Joyce stood in awe of this momentous event.

Mama wrapped a scarf around her head and put on woolen gloves, and my friend Leona bundled up in her fur coat and hat. I carried my box of treasures and held it on my lap while Mama, Leona, and I rode on the Diversary Avenue street car to 1044 Francisco Avenue. Once There, Mama proudly announced to the receptionist, "This is my daughter, Margaret, and she is going to be a nurse." Then they were gone. I was alone in a large room with two metal beds, two small metal dressers, two metal desks, and one closet.

For a long time I looked at the dresser and wondered if I would ever fill three dresser drawers---and I wondered who had my drawer at home. Carefully I put my Bible and devotional book on the desk, and then hung up my skirt and blouses; the rest went in one drawer. The mystery package was homemade fudge made by Grace, with all the sticky fingers licking the pan. Then I cried! Within a short time my roommate, Hertha, came with father, mother, and brother carrying suitcases---and Danish delicacies for us to have a party.

A friendship that began in high school continued into the new millennium. The day came when I filled the dresser drawers, but the memories have never had enough room.

PS: It took all day to unpack the van and get Katie Elise settled. I'll write her a letter to remind her to make room for the memories.

seven

The Forbidden Fence

"Grammy, I can't believe you went to the far end of the beach to write; it's much too deserted to be alone." "I realize that now, Katie Elise, but we used to play hide and seek in those sand dunes." I said, trying to defend my actions. Then there was the time Benjamin, a cousin, jumped over a forbidden fence and landed in a bed of prickly sand burrs screaming, 'Call an ambulance!' When I leaned over the fence I said, 'You can get back the same way you got there.' 'Help!' he screamed when we put him in the car. Later we pulled the burrs out with tweezers and washed him with warm water and alcohol---then he really screamed! That was the last time he jumped the 'Keep Off' fence."

"It's that way at the beach, Grammy---someone always wants to dare the waves in spite of a 'No Swimming' sign," observed Katie Elise. "The sand burrs of life are there, Katie Elise. If obedience is difficult, just think how difficult disobedience is. Every choice has consequences. Someone said that the great tragedy is to live with forgiven sin: the law of the harvest. We often strike up the band and roll out the red carpet for the prodigals who return home; yes, all heaven rejoices. But I often wonder if we forget to rejoice when the young stay the course and walk in obedience to God's rules. That's when the bands should also play "Amazing Grace'---to be kept by the power of God. Remember Katie Elise, when you go to college and have to make the decisions without family to guide you, that you can depend on the Holy Spirit to whisper 'this is the way'. And obey-- one step at the time. You won't be jumping forbidden fences to land in prickly sand burrs." "I won't forget, Grammy," she replied, then she was gone.

One day when I was having lunch with a young couple I told the story of meeting a homeless man in New York. "He was dressed in a yellow slicker, pockets bulging with food from a nearby church. I introduced myself as 'Margaret' and asked for his name. "My name is Joe," was his quick reply. "Do you have a family?" I continued. "My parents are dead, and the living want nothing to do with me," he said. I couldn't help but wonder what happened to an articulate, handsome middle-aged man. "What happened, Joe?" I couldn't help but ask. "I was a journalist and fell in love with a beautiful woman in Holland. Then she left me---turned me down." We were silent for a moment. I had a mental picture of Huckleberry Finn, from Mark Twain, when he was gliding down a dark river closed in by the blackness of night and said to himself, 'This is a deep loneliness---perhaps the best kind.'

To me Joe was gliding on a dark river of deep loneliness. "Joe," I broke the silence and took his arm; "she made a big mistake. I think you would have been a very interesting man to live with." At that he smiled. "You really think so?" "Handsome, too, I might add." Then he laughed out loud. Silence again. Joe continued, "Sometimes a storm comes up and a tree falls across the road and you have to back up. I backed up too far when the storm came." "Joe," I said, "God is right where you left him; get back on the road and write. God is calling you home---to Him." I hugged him and kissed his whiskered face. "Thank you, Margaret---thank you for talking to me," he said. Then he was lost in the flow of broken humanity.

We continued eating our lunch, and I watched the young couple in front of me. With a sad smile one said, "it doesn't take much to get off the road." I added, "It only takes 'I will' to get back on track." I often wonder about Joe in New York, did he get back? As for the young people I meet, I keep reminding them that the sand burrs of life will keep stinging until they get back on the road. When I was visiting a campus a young man came up to me and said, "Sometimes I feel like we have been put out to pasture with no fences. We probably would jump the fences, but at least we'd have a place to come back to."

eight

The Four Prong Plug

"Dennis the Menace is on the way!" My plans for writing at the beach took a dramatic turn; my direction changed, turning right on College Road to head for Lowe's, the lumber and supply store. Hurricane Dennis was on his way. That January I purchased a generator, determined to be ready for hurricanes or Y2K.

I try to keep an on-going love affair with plumbers and electricians, so I called faithful Walter, the electrician, about my generator. "Wrong generator, I prefer the four prong plug," he stated. "Yes sir!" I always say "yes sir" to Walter; he is the authoritative type, and I feel like a kid in a principal's office. Months passed; warm sunny days of writing and travel stayed in front, and the generator was forgotten. Then the headlines; "Hurricane Dennis Coming Toward the Carolina Coast". I think everyone in Wilmington must have read the headlines because generators were wheeling into the parking lot as fast as credit card bills were signed. All around the aisles were batteries and flashlights, so I just filled my cart. I tried to look intelligent when reading the directions on the generator box. I heard men talking about male and female plugs---I never heard of such a thing! Then there was a discussion about cables.

Finally I asked to speak to the manager. Within a few moments I was introduced to Lee, a handsome man. I thought, "I should keep managers on my list of special friends." Then I humbly explained that I had bought a generator but Walter wanted the four prong plug one---and the generator had been in the garage since January. "No oil or gas in it?" Lee asked. "Oh, no, never been touched." I tried to explain that I like to keep Walter happy. "Just return it; I'll get the new one in your trunk. But we'll have to tie it down, so drive carefully," he cautioned. "Thank you, sir!"

It doesn't hurt to use "sir". Respect goes a long way these days---seems to be little enough around. Since people were reaching for yellow extension cords I was not to be out done, so I put one in my cart. Now the new generator---and the four prong plug. "Sorry, we are sold out!" said the salesman. "Sold out?" "You can call your electrician and perhaps he can find one in a supply house." Walter won't like that! Now Walter is a good man; he comes when I call, even if it is some insignificant item. But I know he will remind me that I had a year to get ready for hurricanes. With the new four plug generator tied down in the trunk I just smiled at the stares in the traffic and kept in the lane; I took no shortcuts and stuck to traffic lights.

When I pulled into the driveway it started to rain; I wondered how I would get the generator out of the trunk, when I happened to see some college students loading surfboards. I put on my most helpless look. "Could you big strong men help a grandma? See that generator?" They saw! With flexed muscles and that macho look they hauled the generator into the garage. "Anytime, anytime---no problem!" I guess I'll bake a chocolate cake. When I dialed Walter's number his patient wife answered and suggested that I get certain identification numbers so Walter wouldn't have to make an extra trip. It didn't work! All my numbers were wrong, and I didn't know anything about male and female plugs. "Are you up early?" he asked. "Oh yes, I'll be up!"

At 7 a.m. the next morning I plugged in the coffee pot and sent the dog outside; then the doorbell rang. I ran to the door, forgetting my robe. There I stood in a sheer nightgown and long white hair flying in all directions---I must have looked like a witch. He gave one look and said, "I came to see the generator." I ran for my bathrobe, locked Scarlet in the den, and headed for the garage. He wrote down numbers and muttered male and female, but I wasn't about to show my ignorance. I was in enough trouble. You've had since January to get ready." he stated. "I know---I'm sorry." "Where's your grandson?" "He's at a wedding in Boone, North Carolina." "Humph!!!" It was then I put on my most intelligent face and added, "I remembered to get the cord." Walter had that principal look again; he raised his bushy eyebrows. "Wrong cord! Get your money back, and I'll get the cord---not taking any chances." "Do you have a roller for the generator?" "Oh yes!" At last I did something right! "We'll roll it close to the door in the garage and use the extension cord to plug it in a receptacle I'll make. Then you turn off the main switch and only use the generator for emergency measures---one room and the refrigerator. If you do it wrong, you can blow up everything!" He looked at me like I had already blown everything, and then added, "I hope I can get back to you before the hurricane." "Oh thank you, Walter, and I'm sorry I'm so much trouble." When the van pulled out I caught what he had said: "I hope I can get to you *before* the hurricane." Dennis, you better stay out to sea! Thinking about the possibility of Walter returning, I cleaned out the garage to make room around the generator---there would be no break in our friendship. I even found a fan to blow on him when he returns to work in the hot garage. In the middle of all the pulling and shoving and sweeping I managed to slide the generator on a rug---closer to the door---at least I had learned that trick.

A call came from my friend Inez in Seattle. When she asked what I was doing I sat down in the garage and told her the entire story. We laughed together on the phone. (It sounds so ridiculous; I might just put it in a book!) "Whatsoever things are good---think on those things." A laugh is good! By the time I moved, pushed, and loaded up the garbage can I was dirty from head to toe. So I jumped in the shower, then stretched in Harold's chair to hear the weather report: "Dennis creeping slowly---probably hit Sunday".

I was so tired I couldn't care less about plugs (male or female), extension cords, or even hurricanes. I made a banana sandwich---toast, mayonnaise, and sliced bananas---nothing like it. "Come on, Scarlet, I've had it!" (In case you couldn't reach me between two and three---I had the phone off the hook and stretched out on the den sofa to take a nap.) All my bones and muscles were rattling around to get in place, but before I could figure it out I fell asleep, with Scarlet on the floor beside me. After an hour, Scarlet nudged me: "Enough is enough." The phone went back on the hook. It was then I remembered the caramel sauce Jan brought from Alaska, so I just did it---made a caramel sundae, sat down in the breakfast room, and watched the clouds gather in the sky. During the last hurricane we had twelve people, four dogs, and two cats---and lived! Now I had stocked the shelves: ham for Sunday, corn on the cob, green beans, cantaloupe, and chocolate cake---it's Sarah's birthday. Hopefully we'll have power to get everything prepared early, in case Walter doesn't make it. A generator stands in the garage with stored power---a four prong plug missing.

nine

Dear Jan

August 30, 1999

Dearest Jan,

There is too much static on our phone line so I'll just tell you we are fine---and write the details. Believe me, with all my preparation for this hurricane I earned an "A" for effort. Our new pastor Bill, his wife June, and Uncle Peter joined us for Sunday dinner and Sarah's birthday party. Conversation around the table centered on hurricanes in the past, but I assured them that I was ready for anything. By the way---Walter came, but unfortunately it was when I was on the phone with you on Saturday. I remember hearing Scarlet barking, but I thought it was Buddy, the yard man---who didn't show up, by the way. Later, when the phone rang it was Walter. 'Where were you?" "Oh no! I was on the phone. Then I discovered the doorbell doesn't work, so I guess I need a new doorbell." I could tell Walter was taking a deep breath. Then a sigh came. "That won't be done for a while." "Oh, yes sir, just whenever you can get to it." "Get a pen and write down these instructions:

1. Turn off the main switch.

2. Plug the cord with the white line into the receptacle beside your unit.

3. Fill with gasoline and motor oil.

4. Start up the generator.

5. Only turn on the ones I marked--refrigerator and kitchen.

6. Remember this is just an emergency measure.

7. Leave the garage door partly open for fumes to escape.

8. Do not ever have your main unit and generator on at the same time.

"I left the right cord outside the fence---didn't want to tangle with that Doberman." said Walter. I felt like Moses getting the Ten Commandments, so I wrote down two sets of directions---just in case I died and went to heaven, so the family wouldn't blow the place up. In fact, everyone memorized the directions---even the guests. I gave them the grand tour to see this generator, and I think it was Pastor Bill who suggested that I ought to get it out of the box first. I think that was supposed to be a joke, but nothing about that generator is funny. On the table beside the generator I have a bag full of batteries and various flashlights---one for each room. I was taking no chances!

By the time Bill and June heard about our hurricanes (they had just moved from Montreat, North Carolina, land of the Blue Ridge Mountains) they were ready to go home and board up their new home. Ralph stayed glued to the weather channel; Chris and I took our Sunday nap. Dennis kept creeping closer to shore. The woods in back of the house soaked up the rain and moaned with the wind. "I suggest we go to the concert at church since it hasn't been canceled. I'm tired of watching this unpredictable Dennis." Ralph announced. We braved the rain and wind and joined about five hundred people who decided that if the musicians could come, we should support them. It was one of those family night affairs of happy Southern gospel music. For two hours the wind and the rain were forgotten while a joyous crowd entered into a foot tapping, hand clapping Southern style camp meeting. The beautiful Presbyterian church echoed with the sounds of another day. I voted our own quartet number one when they sang *"the blood will never loose its power"*, then did a beautiful rendition of *"because He lives I can face tomorrow"*.

Chris and Ralph went home to check their situation. I drove down College Road---no back roads in this rain---and made it safely to my driveway. Before I went inside I pulled the garbage can into the garage. The wind could scatter the contents everywhere. I had visions of banana peelings canoeing down a flooded street. When I completed the routine chores of getting ready for bed, Scarlet and I sat down to watch the weather channel. By midnight I had had it with Dennis, churning along the coast and tormenting everyone. All the beach residents had evacuated. The power was turned off; only the police were left to patrol the area. Anyone returning over the bridge had to wear identification as beach residents. I talked this over with Scarlet and called Ralph to tell him I was fine and they should wait until morning to leave their home on the sound. "Old girl, I think we've had a day of it." I told Scarlet. So we made the rounds---locked the doors, turned on night lights. Then I reached for the flashlight to keep beside my bed---four flashlights and NO batteries. In the garage I had a table full of flashlights and batteries still sealed in those impossible packages. "How do you like that, Scarlet? I worked for three days to get ready for this Hurricane Dennis---and no flashlight." For a moment we opened the back door and looked into the sheets of rain between me and the garage door. Scarlet turned away---a definite clue for me not to get soaking wet in my robe and slippers. So I locked the door and decided to get a big candle and a box of matches for the bathroom. I was too tired to do one more thing, so if push came to shove I could light my way by candlelight and retrieve those flashlights. (I'm not sure how to put batteries in, but I guess I'll learn.)

"Scarlet, let me tell you something. It's not always the big crisis in life that throws a curve. Somehow we brace ourselves for the big ones, but then some dumb thing like four prong plugs and batteries can throw your world upside down. Let's go to bed!" Scarlet curled up with her blanket in the laundry room. I could tell she was fed up with all the comings and go-ings and, like me, welcomed the routine of the ordinary. With a prayer of thanks to God for his mercy I fell asleep hugging my down pillow---and missed the hurricane. Since I was over-drawn on energy I slept until 8 a.m. I dared to look outside, where debris littered the landscape---but the power was on! My candle in the bathroom will stay there.

The news report was that thirty percent were without power. Ralph and Chris were part of that number. They called to say "we're on our way for breakfast". (Before I could call you, Jan, my phone was out of order.) With a thankful heart I opened the door for Scarlet and gave her some encouragement to face the wind and rain. I explained that this was an emer-gency and pushed her out the door. Within a few minutes I was on breakfast alert and the kitchen had the delightful aroma of sizzling bacon, fried new potatoes, and a pan ready for eggs and cheese. Six slices of buttered toast went into the oven to get that crisp texture only the oven can bring. With the shades pulled up in the breakfast room I saw Ralph's beautifully craft-ed round table as the perfect setting. My flower beds are bend-ing low, but when the sun comes out they will rise again. The car door slammed in the driveway. "Guess what, Mom? We slept through the storm---never knew the power was off. So here we are!" said Chris. This was just the day for a country breakfast---except I didn't bake biscuits. Oh well, I can't do everything.

There's something about a round table that makes you linger a while. We went from conversation about hurricanes to theological issues: the will of God, the will of man, the sovereignty of God, choices we make. It seems that in the dead-end crises in my life I have been reminded of a favorite hymn:
"All the way my Savior leads me
What have I to ask beside?
Can I doubt his tender mercy
Who through life have been my guide?"

We went back over the years to when a fifteen minute interview with Les Stobbe brought me into the family of Here's Life Publishers with my first book, First We Have Coffee. Ralph recalled challenges that would seem right--then would come a closed door. But when he bought his lovely home on the sound, four different sales, involving four people, had to culminate at the right time, but it finally became their lovely home on the sound. Like pieces in a jigsaw puzzle the deals fit in place--God's timing.

Once again I was reminded of the fact that all of God's redemptive power moves on the track of our obedience to Him. *"Trust and obey---no other way!"* Ralph read Psalm 42 and thanked God for his protection. Then he went to check on his shop, the Master's Touch. I had a room full of flashlights---no batteries. Jesus said, "I am the light of the world"--and if we open our heart's door to Him, He will come in and shine through us. Without Him we are hollow flashlights without batteries.

Love,
Mother

ten

Dear Katie Elise

September 1, 1999

Dearest Katie Elise,

I know you wanted to be here to greet Dennis, but for some wonderful reason (prayer?) a barrier came up and kept the hurricane along the shoreline---not a direct invasion. My phone service is disrupted, but I still have electrical power, so I write to you instead of calling. At least you were tucked away in the mountains, safe and secure. You were definitely in the middle of hurricane Fran two years ago when we had twelve people, four dogs, and two cats! The ocean came up to your front steps, and Shawn had left his clothes in the flooded basement, so ten loads hit my faithful washing machine. Then the showers were kept busy for others who had no power. We emptied freezers and ate what we had in storage. What I remember the most is the blueberry cobbler we made with Horace and Tennie Hilton's blueberries, since they had to evacuate the beach. Aunt Jeanelle and Uncle Peter were here, and that was the last hurricane for my beautiful sister. Now she is Home---no tears or hurricanes. I read some place that we brace ourselves to meet the big crises in life but can fall apart over a trivial incident.

Chad answered my phone with "home for the homeless and animal shelter". I took it all in stride: organizing meals, keeping animals separated, washing machine running all day, and all the coming in and going out. Then I blew it! The Hiltons were asleep in my air conditioned office, Ralph and Chris asleep in the guest room, boys in the garage. Some of you were watching a program, and I peeked in to say good night after coming out of the shower. Big mistake! That was the moment I really "blew my cool", as Chad would say. You, my angel Katie Elise, were holding a stray cat---with a diaper on the cat! I let out a yell. "Katie Elise! Another cat!" "He was so pitiful," you pleaded. "So am I---pitiful. I'm exhausted and don't need more stray cats!" I stomped off to bed---oh yes I did---and forgot all about "don't let the sun go down on your wrath". The sun had long gone down and I was furious, feeling sorry for me. "You feel sorry for a cat---why don't you think of poor old Grammy!" Then I couldn't sleep because I felt sorry for the poor old Grammy, not the silly cat---with a diaper, no less! It took some time, Katie Elise, before I got over feeling sorry for poor old Grammy. Then I did say I was sorry for losing my cool over a cat---diaper or no diaper. Instead of feeling sorry for a kitten in a storm I felt sorry for a Grammy who felt "used" and taken advantage of in a crisis.

I'm telling you this, my dear Kathie Elise, to say that not everything is worth going to the wall for---not even the cat! I'm sorry I reacted instead of just going to bed, sleeping on it, then discussing later about asking permission and not taking things for granted. There is always a right way and a wrong way to handle situations, and I used the wrong way. You already know I was sorry about that.

By the way---I'm enclosing an article about "attitude" written by Chuck Swindoll. He reminds us that ten percent is what happens to us and ninety percent is how we react. "We can't change the past, but we can play on that one string---our attitude." That's good for you and me, Katie Elise. I must tell you the flashlights are ready, because I dumped all the flashlights on the table---with the mix and match batteries---right in front of your daddy. So now I have flashlights for several rooms. So much for that!

It's amazing how small things can upset our well-laid plans---like the day I lost it over a cockroach. When that cockroach streaked across my cabinet I let out a bloodcurdling yell and dumped kitchen drawers on the table. My old knees don't take to crawling behind the lower cabinets, so I called your mother. "Help! Chris!" Not just my old bones needed adjusting, but my attitude needed altering. On the other hand, you saw the entire affair as an adventure. Believe me, you were much younger then and perhaps don't even remember when you crawled behind the closed cabinet doors and went prowling for dinosaurs with a flashlight. When you discovered a dinosaur you shouted for joy. I yelled in fury! You had fun---I fumed! Then you scrubbed the shelves and poured baking soda in the corners. (Someone said it works---and it seemed to.) I really didn't care if those roaches had indigestion---but believe me, I did! My plans took a detour that day, but you made it fun---and I'm still remembering it. Keep that attitude, Katie Elise, and you will do well in college. And if I'm tempted to "lose my cool" I'll remember you hunting dinosaurs. The phone service has just been restored, so hopefully I can keep you posted by phone. Not having a phone is quite disruptive, but it didn't get me upset---I just wrote a letter instead. Always remember, Katie Elise, the line is always open---call collect.

Love,
Grammy

P.S.---God always accepts collect calls too.

eleven

Fried Onions

Fried green tomatoes made a good movie, and I'm wondering if I could do something with "Fried Onions". My friend Billie and I decided to have a luncheon for twenty special friends of long standing. That was the time I did something smart---wheeled my car to Sam's Wholesale and bought chicken pot pies. Billie did the work of cutting up fresh fruit in an antique bowl. It looked like a picture from *Southern Living*. Billie called. "My cakes fell last night, so I had to bake two chocolate chip cakes this morning---but I'll be right there." I finished up a plate of deviled eggs, checked the table and flowers, and looked at the spotless kitchen. Then I headed for the shower.

A car door slammed! "Hi, Grammy. I'm hungry!" It was the familiar voice of Shawn, my grandson. "Just drop some frozen waffles in the toaster---don't mess up my kitchen!" When I stepped out of the shower the aroma of burnt onions greeted me. "Oh no! I can't believe this!" Smoke and burnt onions filling my perfect kitchen! "No problem, Grammy. I'll clean up and spray Lysol around." "Shawn, I do believe there is a law against strangling your grandson, but I am about to break the law."

While I dressed hurriedly Shawn was busy mixing an omelet with everything he could find in the refrigerator. About that time the guests arrived and exclaimed, "Oh, what smells so good?" There stood Shawn grinning from ear to ear, giving his special recipe to my attentive guests---and he did it with his grandfather's charm. I couldn't strangle a hero! When Billie came with the warm chocolate cakes and fruit I almost had to handcuff that grandson. "Stick to your omelet and burnt onions---enough trouble for one day." Billie slipped him a bowl of fruit to go with the omelet, but I grabbed the deviled eggs just in time.

Needless to say we had a good time, and the Sam's chicken pies went over big time! Whew! That was easy! The chocolate cake melted in our mouths. But the best came when we shared stories about trips and sang the old songs with Peter Stam at the piano. When Horace Hilton, the beloved pastor, closed with a blessing, we knew that old friends of long standing had been touched by an angel. Billie and I are working on another luncheon---maybe Christmas---and I'll go back to Sam's for more chicken pot pies. No more burnt onions!

My days of ordinary routine don't last long because there seems to come exclamation points to bring me to a screeching halt. "You won't believe what I did today," beamed Shawn. "Oh no!" The memory of fried onions still lingered in my memory. "I sang in the St. James Episcopal choir," he added. "You did what?" I asked in shock. "I knew you'd be impressed." "Impressed! What's wrong with singing in your own church?" "Well, my friend James is the soloist and extended an invitation to hear him sing. Then he suggested that I try out for the choir. I'm a bass, Grammy." "I'm impressed!" "I put on a robe and marched in with the choir singing 'A mighty fortress is our God, a bulwark never failing'. It was awesome! The anthems are all scripture---beautiful! It's great to try something new." I shook my head. Burnt onions, omelets---now singing at St. James. What next?

Later in the week I attended a luncheon where a lovely guest commented on the beautiful music at St. James, then added, "Such handsome young men in the choir." I couldn't resist. "Well, one of those handsome young men is my Presbyterian grandson who enjoys singing in your choir." "Oh my, he passes by my pew when the choir marches in." (I hope she pinches him.)

twelve

The Stubble and the Wheat

After the hurricane a gentle calm settled in. The ocean rolled peacefully, the seagulls crested the waves for fish, and the sun smiled from a cloudless sky. Looking out over my flower gardens I knew it was time for action when the weeds were as tall as my plants. With grim determination I donned a new outfit for the garden. The paint splattered polyester shorts had seen enough warfare and landed in the garbage can. From the bottom drawer I pulled out bright red shorts and a tee-shirt from one of my women's retreats that had in bold black letters "A Day of Renewal". With a green bandana around my head and gloves and hoe I was ready for business. The weeds had shown their colors, standing tall and bold in my flower bed as though they belonged. It didn't take long to establish "plants rights", and those weeds, roots and all, were tossed out of my garden. Gentle rain during the night had made the earth soft and pliable so the weeds came out easily.

My "Day of Renewal" tee-shirt reminded me it was time to sit on the porch swing and get renewed for the next round. Scarlet sat beside me while I sipped cold water and looked over the work---and it was good. "Well, Scarlet, I guess it worked out for the best that I waited until the weeds grew tall and were easily identified." While I carry on these conversations I brush her coat. No one can accuse me of talking to myself---I have an attentive audience.

Looking over the garden I was reminded of a parable in the Bible about a man who planted a field of wheat. Then one of the servants was upset because someone, probably an enemy, had sown stubble with the wheat. Now wheat is the grain of a cereal grass, providing flour for bread, but stubble and unidentified weeds, that grow amongst the wheat, needs to be destroyed. The farmer decided to let the stubble and wheat grow together until harvest; then the wheat would fill the barns and the stubble would be burned.

Sometimes I think the grandchildren should hear these profound thoughts that I express out loud to Scarlet. But then it takes little to make her happy---just the sound of my voice is enough. I found myself swinging and singing an old tune:
I come to the garden alone
While the dew is still on the roses
And the voice I hear
Falling on my ear...

I stopped! Am I listening? He walks with me and He talks with me? Even in the garden? At the far end of the yard there was another flower bed that needed "plant rights" established. That's where I kept an old chair to encourage my "Day of Renewal". There was the story of the old lady rocking in her chair: "Sometimes I sets and thinks, then again, sometimes I just sets." When I finished the renewal of the garden---and me---I decided to bring this day to a close and retreat to my favorite place, Harold's leather chair.

Evening is that time of day when birds go to their nests and the squirrels stop their play, while shadows steal over the flower beds. It is also that time of day when memories come on slippered feet to recall the times of family laughter, tears, or sorrow---when life was shared with loved ones. Somehow it doesn't seem right that many women are left to carry the burdens of the day alone. But they are there---faithfully praying for the lost and straying, reaching out when help is needed, trusting God to keep them safe and show forth his love to the next generation. When evening comes and we close the blinds on the outside world, we shed our quiet tears. But not for long, for hope springs up in knowing that joy comes in the morning. Even Scarlet knows those "missing you" kind of evenings and gets as close to Harold's chair as she can wiggle. Then she puts her head in my lap and without words say, "I am here". When listening to the news I couldn't help but think about the wheat and stubble; it seemed that wickedness in high places seemed to choke out the wheat.

It was then I remembered my time in Birch Hills, Saskatchewan, where my Papa pitched the tent---over seventy years ago. When the wheat was harvested, small fires were seen across the barren fields. "oh, we have to burn up the stubble---clogs up the machinery" said the farmer. What stubble is clogging up the machinery of my life?

In response to mail regarding hate crimes Ann Landers published a piece written by Sam Levinson in 1981. He listed some of the accomplishments the Jews had made to our world of medicine: Jonas Salk---Polio vaccine; Blumberg---vaccine for hepatitis, A. V. Wasserman---Wasserman test for syphilis; Ehrlick---drug to fight syphilis; Bela Schick---diphtheria test; Minkawski---insulin; B. Crohn---Crohn disease; Alfred Hess---Vitamin C; C. Funk---Vitamin B. From London came the news about a Dr. Eichengruen; who discovered aspirin, but because he was Jewish the credit was given to someone else. During these times of great discoveries the stubble of wickedness, evil, and hatred were also growing. When he was seventy-five Eichengruen's chemical plant and most of his wealth was seized and he was sent to a concentration camp. What irony to think of all the wicked men taking aspirin for their headaches when a genius sat in a death camp.

The mystery of evil comes in dark clouds of despair to join with the unanswered questions of suffering until we can feel ourselves drifting out on a sea of confusion, to crash against the rocks of unbelief and cynicism.

Philip Yancey suggested taking the "magnifying glass of our faith and focus on Jesus Christ". Looking at Jesus restores a renewed vision and we can see a righteous Judge of all the earth bring in the harvest of wheat and destroy the stubble. Long after the smoking furnaces, the clanging chains, and the marching boots fade into the past there will also be the memory of a silent church. The bell tolls for the death of outrage in a bygone day. Will it toll for America?

Then there was the "wheat" that grew---an underground church---and men like Dietrich Bonhoffer chose to stand with the faithful rather than be safe in America. Dohnanyi, dying of diphtheria, was carried on a stretcher to his execution. April 9, 1945, Bonhoffer was hanged for high treason, a month later the Third Reich came to an end.

Corrie Ten Boom's family perished in the concentration camp, but Corrie lived to proclaim that there is no pit so deep but that God's love can reach the depth. Bonhoffer's last reading was: "Blessed be the God and Father of our Lord Jesus Christ. By His great mercy we have been brought into a living hope." The wheat lives!

It had been a long day of stubble and wheat. The shades were drawn, the night came to enfold us in the comfort of sleep. "Oh God, let us be like trees planted by the living water, to grow fresh and green in the midst of the stubble of the world." Scarlet was tucked away in the laundry room with her blanket, and I reminded her that another hurricane was on the way. "It's always that way, Scarlet. You get through one crisis in life, and then there is a time of calm. Then out of the blue comes another crisis. Like Harold used to say, "We aren't made in a crisis---a crisis reveals what we are."

thirteen

The Uprooted Dream

My childhood memories of the Canadian prairie had placed a dream of a farm deep inside me. I drew up plans for the farm: for cows and chickens, gardens and flowers, shade trees and swings, verandas and rocking chairs. Then crashing into my dream came the nightmare of war in Vietnam! By this time Janice Dawn, our first-born, was happily married to Judson Carlberg. Our younger son, Ralph, was in school. Harold traveled throughout many of the eastern and southern states, and I was the infirmary nurse at Greensboro College. With tears in our hearts, Harold and I had watched our lanky, blue-eyed Dan, our elder son, board a train in Raleigh. Destination: Vietnam. "Don't worry about me, Mom," he had told me. "I have the armor of God over my army uniform. I'll be home again!" With a chug of its engine and a clang of its wheels, the train pulled away.

It was Sunday morning, and we found ourselves driving teary-eyed toward church. During the communion service someone sang, "Fill my cup, Lord. I lift it up, Lord..." I felt drained and empty; doubt fought to remove the faith I struggled to keep. Yet soon God's peace quietly filled my cup and

His love enveloped me in His presence. I was in a safe place.

While letters and packages flew across the miles, I marked the days on a calendar. Each month I embroidered a square for a quilt, marking Dan's year in Vietnam; each square had a message of hope. My journal began to fill up with God's promises. *All thy children shall be taught of the Lord; and great shall be the peace of thy children. (Isaiah 54:13) I will contend with him that contendeth with thee, and I will save thy children. (Isaiah 49:25)*

Lena Rogers Leach, the beloved maid who worked with me in the infirmary at Greensboro College, joined me in the battle to believe. Lena, with her shiny ebony skin and wide, dark eyes, had fought more than one spiritual battle for the college students at Greensboro. Now her heart of love included my sons. The battle was fought not only for Dan in Vietnam, but also for Ralph. He was held hostage by the enemy in a war zone of rebellion against God's authority. Location: New England. Dan's war was fought with guns and tanks; the war for Ralph, a spiritual war, was not fought with conventional weapons but with the sword of the Word of God and the shield of faith. My dream of a farm was held suspended between these two wars.

Then in November 1969 Dan came home. For Dan the war was over. He came home with a dream---like mine---a dream of a farm where all the family could come for reunions, or even to live. While Dan taught school in the mountains, he drew up plans. "Just listen to that child talk!" Lena threw back her head and laughed joyously as she listened to Dan spill out his dream and said, "Families should not be separated. That's what our child says. God never intended folks to be torn apart. Lord, have mercy! Dan thinks Lena is coming to that farm to cook cornbread and fry chicken for all the Jensens coming down the road!" Lena and I plastered pictures of farms all over the kitchen wall of the college infirmary. "We have the farm in our heads. Now all we need is some land to put it on," Lena chuckled. Laughter filled the infirmary kitchen and hope flooded our hearts. Lena folded her arms across her ample bosom. "That's not all---our child Ralph is coming home. God done told us that. Now we just wait to see how God works his plan out. We just trust and obey."

One day Lena bought a newspaper on her way to the college. Over a cup of coffee she and I began our Bible study and prayer. Then Lena opened the paper. "Look at this, Nurse Jensen. This could be Dan's land for sale---sixty-six acres near Stoneville, a small town thirty miles from here. Just wait till Dan comes from school and we show him this paper." Lena got a beat, then hummed a tune; soon the words came:

Go out there, Dan,
Possess the land.
We move one step at the time.
We walk by faith,
Not by sight.
We move one step at the time.
The Word's a lamp;
The Word's a light.
We move one step at the time.
We walk by faith,
Not by sight.
We move one step at the time.

We had our theme song!

Then Ralph came home! Our tall, lean son---our handsome, southern blue-eyed boy---had gone off to a Christian college but with the seeds of rebellion already stirring inside him. We almost lost him to the quicksands of sin. He came back as a stranger---gaunt, bearded, long-haired, hunched over in his fleece-lined jacket. Then in the midst of the rebellion, God worked his miracle in Ralph's life, turning him around and really bringing him home---home to God, home to us. The war had been won and heaven and earth rang with "Amazing grace! How sweet the sound!" It was September 15, 1970.

Dan's new farm near Stoneville now was expanding to include a place for the boys' hippie friends to come for food and lodging. With machete in hand, Ralph carved a path through the brush to the gurgling spring. Dan bulldozed the scrub fields and made a pasture for Ginger, the horse---and perhaps the wobbly legged calves I saw in my dream. Together we planted fruit trees and gardens while the valley rang with the sound of saws and hammers.

The log cabin at our farm was replaced with a chalet-type house, which Harold and Dan designed and built. It had cedar siding and open beams. A wide stairway brought us to the second and third floors where the view stretched to hazy blue mountains and Hanging Rock, a favorite scenic ridge. One by one, Ralph's old friends came to see what had happened to Ralph and if, indeed, he was a new creation. They saw the valley and stayed; later, they saw the miracle of God's love.

Guitars strummed into the night, accompanied by whip-poorwills calling to each other while stars watched. "Families shouldn't be separated," Dan had said. Lena nodded. "Too much hurt in the world. Folks need each other and a place to come to---a time for healing from this hurting world. Why, Dan child, you be like Moses fixing to bring us all into the Promised Land." Lena's laughter rang out while we watched the lodge develop and the land, overgrown with scrub trees and weeds, bloom into a beautiful valley of flowers and gardens.

After Harold helped Dan acquire the sixty-six acres, Harold and I purchased the adjoining thirty-eight acres. Across the valley, Doris and David Hammer, my sister and her husband, built their beautiful home overlooking the valley. Across their road stood the yellow house built for our Norwegian Mama and Papa. But Mama came alone. Papa never saw the desk and books in his new study. God took him home to meet the Author of his faith---and the authors of his treasured books.

Dan marked off building sites. Jan and Jud would have a place to build a house or a cabin for summer vacations and even for their retirement in years to come. There would be room for relatives on plots of ground in our combined acreage. My dreams soared. All my life I had moved from place to place, never close to anyone I could call my own. As a child I envied my friends with relatives, so I called older friends "aunt" or "uncle". Now Uncle Howard, Uncle Jack, and the sisters could all come. No one would ever be lonely again. Doris and Dave had 150 acres. Combined, Dan and Harold and I had more than a hundred acres. My brother Gordon from New York bought adjoining property. For five years our family poured strength, creativity, and money into our dream. Dan's chalet neared completion, and our house was sited on a knoll. No one would be separated again. "We all need a place to come home to," Willie from the children's home had told Mama, years ago. I was confident that love would cover the valley with a blanket of peace.

Late into the night we sat around the dining room table in the house on Bethel Spring Dale in Greensboro and ideas flowed on paper as well as through excited conversation. We called Highway 220 North, the Glory Road, as our cars brought food, supplies, and people to our Promised Land. One guest, an artist, watched the valley from the third floor of the lodge. "I'll just bring my canvas and put all this in permanent color," he said. "That's not all; I'll come up here and write books about all that's going on." I answered, "You paint the dream with oil, and I'll paint it with words." We laughed together. The blending of a dream makes a joyful sound. "Missionaries on furlough should have their own home, a place where they can spend time with their families and where they can share in Bible study and prayer with other families," I suggested.

"We need recreational facilities---tennis courts, and a swimming pool," Ralph insisted. "Even a lake, stocked with fish." The ideas flowed like mountain steams, fresh and challenging. Dan named the place Shalom Valley Farm, the place of peace and wholeness. Shalom Valley was carved in wood and etched in our hearts.

And then, suddenly, before the chalet was completed, the dream was gone! Our sky turned black for us. Thunder rolled, and in fury a cold wind swept darkening clouds across the valley. The trees bent in sorrow, and the valley seemed to weep while the uprooted dreams perished in the storm of life. Today the unfinished lodge, still empty, stands alone on its sixty-six acres: "FOR SALE" the sign reads. The wind slaps against the windows, seeking an entrance. The fruit trees we planted are withered, and the fruit on the vines has died. The wild grasses grow again over the valley, and the lonely cry of the whippoorwills call into the night. Standing guard over the lonely house, towering pines reach to the skies, and the valley sobs out its sorrow.

The dreams are dead, and the song is not sung. "Where are you, Lord?" I cried over the valley in the day of destruction. "No! No! My dream can't die! The music can't die now! For fifty years I've held this dream in my heart. No, no---not now---not when it finally seems to be coming true. Now it is gone!" My anguish was unbearable. "We prayed, believed, walked, and worked together step by step. And Lord, it was such a good dream---it really was---and a blessing to so many people. Why, Lord?" Sometimes God answers in silence. This was one of those times. God was silent!

And so it came to pass that Dan went away. He took his beautiful bride to follow another dream---somewhere in the West---where they would build their own little nest. And our dream of a farm for the family was uprooted. And then it also came to pass that Harold said, "Come, Margaret. I believe it is God's will that we move to Wilmington," and Ralph said, "Come, Chris, for when God closes one door, He opens another." He did!

Many months later, after the sharp pain had faded somewhat and turned to a dull ache that never goes away, Harold and I returned to Shalom. On a hazy fall day we walked hand in hand down the overgrown path to stand beside the foundation Ralph had begun for his home. The furniture shop was to have been down by the spring. We looked at the knoll where we had marked off our house. My sister Doris and I had laughed about each having a flagpole so we could hoist a signal when the coffee pot was on. We had said, "When our house sells in Greensboro, then we'll begin to build on Shalom." We wondered why our house didn't sell then---but God knew. God had a plan. Later, long after the weeds had grown back at the farm, when Harold said we should go to Wilmington, the first person who looked at our Greensboro home bought it. God's timing! The valley was gold and red. A quiet peace covered the land. Harold and I wept as we stood beside the empty lodge that Harold had helped to build---three years of his hard work. We could hear again the hammers and saws, the laughter, and the songs from our "hippie boys". We loved them "as is"---God changed them "as His".

Doris and Dave's colonial house still stands high on the hill overlooking the silent valley of Shalom. My brother Gordon died before he could come to his place. And the wind blows through Dan's unfinished lodge. I remember a verse I had written in my journal when I first saw the land: *"A land which the Lord thy God careth for; the eyes of the Lord thy God are always upon it, from the beginning of the year unto the end of the year."* (Deuteronomy 11:12) We turned to look again at the valley with its patchwork quilt of gold, yellow, and red. The towering pines swept the sky---strong, green, and unbending. When we closed the gate, we wiped our tears and left the lodge---so alone---in the setting of God's surrounding beauty. "Keep your eye on it, Lord, please keep your eye on it." A dream was marked "FOR SALE". We didn't go back again!

Now, twenty-five years later, I am rocking on the porch of the beach house, still looking for answers about why some dreams die. Harold wasn't here, but the dream of his children coming to the beach was alive. I wondered if he could see them riding the waves or stretched out on a blanket, reading a book. Chris and Jan were laughing together in the kitchen as they set the long picnic table on the porch for supper. Since they seemed to manage without me in the kitchen, I was free to rock on the porch and remember another day...

We were seated around the dining room table at Bethel Spring Dale in Greensboro with my sister Grace. All the family seemed to be talking at the same time, pouring over the drawings of a dream---laughing, shouting approval of new ideas. An air of expectancy filled the night. Grace turned to me. "I love to sit at your table and hear all these wild plans. If nothing comes of it you have still fulfilled a purpose---hope rising to a crescendo of possibilities."

I remember what Corrie Ten Boom wrote: "The process is the plan." Now Grace is Home! Due to illness Grace was unable to live alone in Greensboro, so I brought her to my home in Wilmington where Joyce, Jeanelle, and I could care for her. I seemed to hear Lena say, "Families need to stay together." This was not what I planned, but we were together. Willie had said so long ago that "everyone needs a place to come home to". Grace was home, surrounded by family---sisters, nieces, and nephews; Grace the quiet one, who never married but devoted her life to Christian service and her family. We sat beside her and remembered the accomplishments of her life, but it was the sacrificial gifts of love when we were children that stayed etched on our hearts; a baby doll for the youngest, Jeanelle, a treasured Shirley Temple doll for Joyce; and a dress she made for me during the night hours. She understood our thanks, and a tear glistened on her cheek. Then the day came when she peacefully went Home while we sang the songs of faith. Before that year of 1997 ended Jeanelle went Home while surrounded by the songs of faith. "Come, Lord Jesus,' she whispered.

"Mom, you are a million miles away!" Ralph pulled up a chair, and we rocked together while the seagulls cried over the rolling waves. "Oh, Ralph, was it all in vain? The endless miles between Greensboro and Stoneville, the energy and money that went into a dream---was it for nothing?" Ralph continued to rock, then slowly answered. "It brought me home; the dream brought me home, and my friends came for the dream. We all found God---the place to come Home to." Ralph took my hand. "Come, Mother, the girls are calling us to the table. Dreams don't die, they just fade away to make room for new ones."

fourteen

Score One for Grammy

"Mom, please come with us to Greensboro since this hurricane is a number 4 category and the eye is looking at Wilmington. Three million people have already evacuated," said Ralph.

"Since you live on the sound you have to evacuate, so please go to Peggy and Tom, your friends in Greensboro. Shawn plans to stay with me---and Scarlet," I replied. Before long there were four cars in the driveway. Ralph had moved furniture in the showroom and locked up his shop. Chris had packed suitcases for evacuation while the men boarded up windows. Neighbors around me were boarding up and pulling out of driveways. But not my friend Clara, my neighbor across the street. "We've weathered these storms before, Margaret, and we can watch out for each other," she said. Lloyd, her husband, had the camper equipped with a generator, so we'd have our coffee.

Now Clara is my unflappable neighbor, solid in frame and faith, seldom complaining about the pain that seems to be a constant companion. "If God's eye in on the sparrow I guess He can keep track of us old birds. Besides, I heard of friends who fled a hurricane and ran into a tornado," she advised. As champions of the neighborhood we would "keep watch over our flock by night". Since Ralph and Chris decided to stay, we put a roast in the oven, and then kept the washing machine going (as long as there was power). The men moved anything movable into the garage. Then we waited out the storm.

After our supper we cleared the round table in the breakfast room and brought out our domino game called "Chicken Scratch" or "Mexican Train". Scarlet sat beside Ralph and watched our every move. Shawn kept drawing the storm's movement on a chart. "We are due a direct hit, Grammy" he'd report. A large tree stood in the front yard, a strong tree that had withstood all the previous storms. "That tree worries me--could crash into the front window," said Shawn. "I've been praying over that tree, Shawn, and it could be our protection against the wind. Let the roots be deep, keep it strong, a refuge in the storm," I meant it! The tree stood! By midnight we decided to go to bed while Shawn stayed on the alert to track the unpredictable Floyd. The power went off.

In the morning we gave God thanks for a night of sleep, and then dared to look at the debris the storm caused. It missed a direct hit on us. The moment of truth arrived! No power! No coffee! Time to activate the generator! I had two pots of coffee ready to go---an emergency measure! The flashlights were ready, one in each room, with batteries. Score one for Grammy! Now was the time for the trial run of the famous generator. Scarlet ran in terror and hid in the laundry room. I emerged with two sets of directions and called each one off. Then the generator roared in triumph. When Lloyd our neighbor came we had another lesson in amps and watts and I discovered that it took three thousand watts for my two coffee pots. In no time the coffee pots perked happily.

All of us called back and forth while Shawn kept a score card: three thousand amps for the coffee pots, one thousand for a two-burner hot plate. So it became a comedy show to unplug the refrigerator to plug in something else. We managed not to blow anything up. Walter will be proud!" "Unplug the refrigerator, I'm making an omelet!" Shawn's specialty!

Finally we sat down around the table and gave thanks for God's grace and mercy. The rain turned into a drizzle, then a patch of blue slipped through the clouds. A shout went up when the sun dared to smile through the mist. Shawn worked on omelets, Chris kept the toast going, and I poured coffee. My generator worked! No one seemed to notice, but my halo was shinning. Everyone was too busy listening to the assessment of damage, and it seemed that the flooding was more serious than the wind. Curfew is still in effect, but I think I'll just walk across the street to Clara and tell her all about my survival plan.

Shawn discovered a lake under the house, then hooked up pumps for drainage. I decided to retreat to my office. Then I realized---no heat! Oh, well, the generator worked! And I had two pots of coffee. The debris clean up will wait until tomorrow when curfew is lifted. Calls came from North, South, East and West saying, "We are praying for you." The best survival plan!

Dennis the Menace once said, "Tomorrow comes before I finish with today." Tomorrow came when neighbors worked together to remove the debris, wash taped-up windows, and loaded up trucks to haul debris to the city dump. Ralph, Chris, and Shawn were part of that clean-up brigade, while Sara hosted stranded friends in her small place---cats and dogs included.

Since I could not be driving trucks I knew I could do something, so I studied the "amps" situation and managed to use my two-burner hot plate to sauté onions, mushrooms, and chicken breast pieces in butter. Off went one pan; then I cooked a kettle of potatoes while I gathered salad makings into a bowl and whipped up Grandma Jensen's dressing: mayonnaise, orange juice, and sugar. A bright table cloth covered the round table; in the center stood four large candles that glowed in the bay window. "Not bad," I thought to myself. Juggling the pots and pans, I browned the chicken lightly in the butter and decided to make Harold's favorite---milk gravy seasoned with salt, pepper, and parsley. The brigade returned, hungry and dirty! "Wow! What a pleasant surprise! We thought we'd get stuck with Shawn's omelet again." "Mashed potatoes and milk gravy, Dad's favorite!" "How did you manage?" they asked. "I just studied generators and amps, besides using a little creativity." I was proud of my humility! Even mushrooms! (Chris' favorite.)

It was such fun for me to watch the faces light up after a day of hauling debris to the dump, and I was reminded how the simple pleasures of life become extra-special after a storm. While we are making other plans it seems that the storms of life hit with a vengeance: the loss of loved ones; the surging of doubt that battles against the pillars of our faith; storms of bitterness and unforgiveness that hold a tenacious grip in the mind. The hurricane comes, and we have to deal with it. The four pillars of faith - Face it! Trace it! Brace for the aftermath---then offer praise! Life's storms are like that! We have to face the storm and shout to the wind, "On Christ the solid Rock I stand---all other ground is sinking sand." As we trace a storm through a family or community we ask, "Will my anchor hold?" The anchor is Jesus Christ! That is the number one stake we can drive into the sands of time. Then we can trace the faithfulness of God through all generations and know that God will work the "all things" for good---when we just trust and obey. Oswald Chambers said, "God's redemptive power moves on the track of our obedience to Him." When we brace ourselves to face the debris in our own lives, we cry out, *"Oh search me, oh God, and see if there is a wicked way in me. Cleanse me from every sin and set me free."* (Psalm 139:23-24)

My Norwegian mama had her version. "Oh, ja, it is so simple---just love and forgive, trust and obey, and do what you know to do. It is so simple, just not so easy." The fourth pillar is praise: Like Lena would say, "Praise is like a detergent-cleans out the cob webs of the mind." In everything give thanks! This is the time to go by what we know and not what we see. We see the devastation, but we know the sun will shine again, the birds will sing, the gentle breezes will blow over the battered gardens, and hope will spring up out of despair. While everyone was talking about the storm, munching on cookies and sipping hot tea, I had all these wonderful thoughts---but no one looked in the mood for a sermon. Later, I'll go over to Clara and tell her about my four pillars in the storms of life--- she knows about storms. "Face it, trace it, brace for it, praise. In everything give thanks."

There are times when the lust for power, possessions, or position fogs up the windows of the soul. Then a storm comes along, and the fog is lifted for faith to see what we know. God's wonderful peace comes over the soul. For everything there is a blessing and a season. Right now it was the season for mashed potatoes and milk gravy, for some of life's simple pleasures: the closeness of family, a game of Chicken Scratch, and Ralph's popcorn (done the old way, in a kettle over the electric plate).

fifteen

The Rocking Chair

We lived through three hurricanes and a flood that devastated North Carolina. Out of all the tragic news someone told a story about a gander swirling around in a flooded creek. Rescue efforts failed. Then someone threw a tarp over the struggling gander to aid in the capture, but the gander went swirling down the river---and not on a "Sunday afternoon" cruise. The sheriff's office received a frantic call. "A huge setting hen is in my front yard---with a raincoat, Help!"

As though storms weren't enough, a pipe burst in my office and I was swirling around in water---and no tarp! "Help!" My neighbors came running, and Mildred, my neighbor, was digging in the front yard to find the main cut off. Clara came in her golf cart. "Stay calm, Margaret! Stay Calm! My cholesterol is up!"

I called Alan, my faithful plumber. "Help!" With the help of neighbors we salvaged books and papers. Then Shawn showed up and cut the water off---under the sink in the garage (in fact, under my nose). "Oh, why didn't I know that?" I moaned in shame and despair. "Oh Lord, isn't it enough that I learned about generators, stupid plugs, amps, watts---and now I have to know where "cut offs" are? I'm ready for Elijah's chariot to carry me Home. I feel like the old gander swirling around in water---and no rain coat!"

They came! Alan, the faithful plumber, a suction crew, then the rug expert to cut up the soaked carpet. Fans were set up to blow out the dampness. My office was in a shamble--- just before Christmas, with mail hidden under boxes of books. Scarlet hid in the laundry room---this was too much! While all the "fix it" crews came---adjustors, repairmen, painters, and plumbers---I stayed in the kitchen baking Jule Kake (Norwegian Christmas bread) and cookies, trying to sing "Praise God From Whom All Blessing Flow". I failed to see any blessings flowing---just water! Then I did see! A gentle man pumping out the water said, "Aren't you thankful your office is separate from the house and your kitchen isn't flooded?" "Oh thank you! I never thought of that!" "Just lock up your office and let the fans blow." I did! Now I sang "Praise God" and meant it.

The wonderful Christmas season came and went, the fans kept blowing. Some warm sunny days added to the "blessings". Then the day came when there was new carpet. My office was ready! All was peace and quiet. The Christmas tree was down; ornaments packed in *labeled* boxes were on the top shelf in the garage. (I wasn't going to get into trouble over bathing suits and Christmas ornaments getting mixed up.) Shawn never got around to putting the outside lights up, but after hurricanes, floods, and a river in my office, I just let it go. Not everything is worth going to the wall for.

On one of those peaceful days Jan called, "Mom, what are you doing?" "I'm getting ready to head for the rocking chair that you and Ralph gave me, to let my soul catch up with my body, I've been going through my record collection and playing everything from Beethoven to Boston Pops, Southern Gospel, Montavoni, and music for lovers (my favorite). Believe it or not, I was swinging and swaying to Hawaiian music---no grass skirt, but my apron did fine."

Scarlet retreated to the laundry room---in shock! "What wonderful memories, Jan! Mario Lanzo is singing "Be My Love". Don't want to miss it---Dad's favorite, you know. I hope he's listening." I added. "I love you, Mom!" "I love you, too, my Jan." We hung up.

Since it was too cold for the beach chair I knew the rocking chair would serve the same purpose, and I'll live with the memories that return in living color. Music does that---refreshes the soul. "When I grow too old to dream I'll have you to remember." What a gift! Memory!

It seems like yesterday when Harold and I piled into an old car with our friends Irene and Porter---babies in our laps and a picnic basket in the car trunk. "With someone like you, a pal good and true, we'd like to leave it all behind." We harmonized old love songs and that's what we were doing---not running "away to the west to build a cute little nest"---but heading to the forest preserve to build a bonfire for hot dogs and marshmallows. The babies played in the play pen. We laughed, talked, dreamed until the stars came out; then we packed up the play pen and basket in the trunk of the car while we held our sleepy little ones and sang all the way home. "Red sails in the sunset, way out on the sea, carry my lover home safely to me." Filled with dreams, youth, and adventure we sang in our four-part harmony, "When your hair has turned to silver I will love you just the same; I will always call you sweetheart, that will always be your name."

The car rolled on. "When I grow too old to dream I'll have you to remember..." The babies fell asleep in our arms. We celebrated more than fifty years of dreams. The hair did turn to silver, but the love and songs remained. Now I am the lone voice of that four-part harmony, and I find myself looking for the lights of Home. We'll sing again!

It takes more than sermons from a pulpit. It takes picnics and love songs to hold committed hearts and hands to weather the storms of life. At the close of last Sunday's service a mellow voice sang, "Just as I am, without one plea---oh Lamb of God, I come." Ralph whispered, "I haven't heard that song in years---so beautiful!" That is how we all come! Ralph and the hippies came in the seventies---just as is! God made them as His! That was how the immigrants came in Papa's Norwegian church---"Just as I am". Then who can forget the streams of humanity coming to the fountain of life in the Billy Graham crusade---their "hour of decision". They came 'just as I am". As a six year old child I came "just as I am' with nothing to give---just me. "I want Jesus in my heart." He came! What did I get? God's amazing grace, his salvation, and a lifetime of his faithfulness to all generations. When I sang "come into my heart, Lord Jesus" He came! He stayed! Over 80 years ago--- and He will be there throughout all eternity. What a hope we have!

Stories from the beach chair, memories from the rocking chair. They both have the same ending: "I'm so glad I learned to trust Him---precious Jesus, Savior, Friend. And I know that He is with me, will be with me to the end!"

sixteen

January 2000 Blizzard

The headlines read: "Snow! Schools Closed! Remember the Blizzard of December 1989!" I remembered! Not only did a blizzard cover North Carolina with snow, wind, and ice, but a storm came against our faith as a family. In 1989 a Christmas festival at the University of North Carolina brought Harold and me to a beautiful banquet table. Dressed in velvet and lace I was the "storyteller" of the evening. Then a storm came without warning and I was in a hospital bed, in a hospital see-through gown (not Victoria's Secrets). Cancer! The impassable roads gave Harold the option to stay in the adjoining room while the blizzard blew; only four-wheel jeeps came through the ice and snow. Medical personnel remained at the hospital to hold double shifts. Unaware of anything around me, I drifted in a world of pain---not only to my body, but also to my soul. In more than seventy years I had seldom missed a day of work due to illness--- not even a cold. Now cancer!

Driving through the storm in a red Jeep, Ralph and Chris brought the gift of Christmas---a festive place setting with hot tea and cookies. "Sarah wanted to come, Mom," Ralph chuckled. "She said, 'Why should Mother go when she isn't remotely related to her. I am her granddaughter!'" I lived with that gift for a long time.

Without warning, storms come! The disciples were settled in to cross the Sea of Galilee, for Jesus said, "We are going over to the other side." For some reason He avoided telling them of the interruption of storms. Jesus slept in the boat while the fear terrorized the disciples. That's how I felt. "Where was Jesus when I needed Him---asleep in the boat?" I shivered in paralyzing fear while waves beat around me, suddenly going from strong and healthy to weak---cancer! "Don't you care?" the disciples cried. Jesus stood up in the boat. "Be quiet!" The storm grew quiet. Turning to the disciples He said, "What happened to your faith?" It wasn't the storm that awakened Jesus---it was the unbelief! Jesus knew that unbelief was more dangerous than a storm. They made it safely to the other side. I couldn't see the other side; I only felt the storm---and Jesus was asleep in my boat. Or was he?

There had been many storms in my life: standing in the gap for my children, facing crises with Harold, danger, loss of loved ones. But somehow I could stand with the armor on---the helmet of salvation, the breastplate of his righteousness, loins girt about with truth, the shield of faith, shoes shod with the gospel of peace. I was strong in faith and strong in body. But when pain and weakness made me feel like a "wet noodle" it was difficult to get a handle on the armor. Unbelief awakened Jesus! He sent the Comforter to remind me that when I am weak, I am strong in Him. Gently I was reminded that He had control of the calendar, for "my times are in His hands". Jesus wasn't asleep in my boat---just listening for the faintest call so He could answer. He was there all the time!

More than ten years have passed. Two years after the Blizzard of 1989 another storm came with the cold icy blast of death when, after fifty-three years together, Harold went Home-suddenly-in my arms. "Jesus, where are you? Asleep in my boat?" "Lo, I am with you always---I will never leave you. Harold is Home, safe from the storms, and you must show my power to the next generation."

The "wet noodle" was learning more about the armor--- even for wimps---his strength. Years before my friend Gladys had said, "Everyone around me seems so strong and victori- ous, and I feel like a 'wet noodle'." We chuckled at the time. The phrase stuck because we all have felt like a "wet noodle". But today my friend stands strong, feet planted on the solid Rock---the anchor of the soul.

Through a tragic accident a friend, Rod, plummeted from the role of a high ranking executive to the "wet noodle" in need of help. Was Jesus asleep in the boat? Why didn't he stop the storm before it hit? I have an idea that Jesus just stood up in that boat and said "Be quiet" to all the waves of questions; then there was a quiet peace. "Don't be afraid. I'm in the boat and I'll never leave you. Trust me!" Maybe Jesus whispered, *"I need executives, but I also need weakness---a vehicle for my strength; turmoil---for truth to shine forth; fear---for faith to show like gold."* Through all the storms will come a peace that is beyond natural understanding. The King of kings was once a baby in need of care. The Creator of all the universe fell down, a broken, bruised body; someone else had to carry the cross for Him. On the cross He carried the sin of the world and cried out in triumph, "It is finished!"

Storms of hate around the world have caused millions to die for their faith in Jesus Christ. Then one day it came close to home, in America, where hate crushed out the lives of young people who dared to say, "I believe!" While tumultuous waves of voices were crying out for explanations, reasons, or answers to the senseless tragedy of Columbine, I could just see Jesus standing up in this ship of state, America. "Be quiet! The answers aren't in law books, but in the Book of the law of life!" From the blood of young martyrs I believe the message from the Book, the Bible, will go forth in power---strength and power through weakness."

"I am the Way, the Truth, and the Life!" Through pain, grief, and tears there is coming a new song from broken hearts, a song of victory through God's grace and mercy. Keep singing, Rod, for you said, "Singing fills the empty places of the soul." Keep singing, God's children all over the world; it's time to take the harps from the willow tree and sing the songs of Zion. Keep singing, broken hearts, for the day is coming when the King in all his glory will come, with untold numbers of angels and trumpets, to herald the day when every knee will bow and confess that "Jesus is King of kings and Lord of lords". Just one more mile---and we'll be Home! Let's finish with a song!

seventeen

Five Year Planner

I embarked on a mission to find a five-year planner. I pulled into one parking lot after the other. I went through the doors of Books-A-Million, Barnes and Noble, and the Salt Shaker, where a clerk graciously called various office supply stores to find a five-year planner. The best we could get was an eighteen-month calendar. It was then I noticed that the people in line, with their books in hand, looked at me with raised eyebrows and a question mark expression. "Oh no, I did it again, wrong earrings---different colors. Or maybe my shoes don't match---lipstick on my nose? Oh well, let them stare." So I did the next best thing---smiled and wished everyone a good day, then headed for my car. Then it hit me! What was an eighty-eight year old great- grandmother doing with a five-year planner? I sat in the car and laughed out loud. (I hope no one saw me!) When I returned home I called Jan. "Can't find a five-year planner." "I couldn't find one either, but I ordered two from the Internet---one for you and one for me." And she wasn't laughing.

Her concerns were different when she found out I was scribbling dates from 2001 and 2002 on the back of an old planner. "Mom, you are going to get dates mixed up, planning too far ahead." "Oh don't worry, honey. I told them I would cancel if Jesus comes, so that took care of that!" Then she did laugh! What a thought! Jesus coming again---and He could come! Many expected Jesus to enter the new millennium with a shout and sounding trumpets, but He didn't come that way. Throughout all time people have set dates with expectancy of his return. I still believe in what the angel said: "Don't keep looking up, but get back to work, and just as He went, He will return." Now that's a promise! God keeps his promises. When that day comes suddenly---morning, noon, or night---I have my bags packed and I'm out of here. That is called the Blessed Hope---and what a hope it is! Prison bars won't hold God's child; sickness and pain won't hinder that journey. Peter Stam brought sister Jeanelle's journal to me. She didn't scribble in her journal like I do. (I'm not too sure I want anyone to see mine---too hard to understand without the gift of interpretation.)

As for my youngest sister, everything she did was perfect, even her handwriting. When she dressed "casual" it was like a model coming out of Vogue. Her older sisters looked like we just got off the farm. A gift from Jeanelle was wrapped so beautifully that you didn't want to tear the wrapping and you saved the matching ribbon. No one worried about my packages. "Oh Mom, that's the bag I gave you last year---only this is Christmas and that was a 'Happy Birthday' bag." "Oh well, I have red tissue paper and green yarn---no big deal." "That's okay, Mom. We can always tell your gifts under the tree---Chris and I recognized the bags we gave you." Jan added. Now that would not happen to Jeanelle---no yarn and old bags.

When I opened her journal I saw her in all the pages: teaching God's Word, going on mission trips with Peter, pouring out her love of life, and rejoicing in her family. Throughout the pages wove a letter of love to the Lord she served. Across the pages were prayer requests---specific needs for her loved ones. Then she wrote, "I waited; I listened for God to speak through his Word, a hymn, or a special phrase." Under each request she wrote how she sensed the answer was given to her---through the Word of God. She prayed for wisdom and understanding. Jeanelle was given keen insight and great wisdom. I listened! "My dear Margaret,that is not your concern. Stay in your boundaries." She was right, and when I look back with regret it is usually because I slipped out of my boundaries to "fix it".

She knew what it meant to "wait on the Lord, trust Him, and He will bring it to pass". When we prayed together she ended her prayer, "Come Lord Jesus, as soon as you can." We spoke often of that day when Jesus would come and every knee would bow and tongues would confess Jesus King of kings---a day when God would wipe all tears away. One day Jesus came! It wasn't the way we expected; there were no trumpets sounding, but He came. In a hospital bed in her beautiful home, surrounded by the people she loved---Peter, who lovingly cared for "his angel"; the children, Charlene and Rob; the sisters; Dr. Luke Sampson; Ralph; beloved pastor Horace and his wife Tennie---He came! A silent cry came from out hearts. "Oh God, how can this be? This beautiful wife and mother, teacher of your Word, musician who filled the concert hall with her music. Is this stilled?" Rob, Jeanelle's son, sang "Surely goodness and mercy will follow me, and I will dwell in the house of the Lord forever." Jeanelle spoke. We listened. "Even so, come Lord Jesus." He came! Now her music joins the angelic hosts.

Going through her journal I sensed God's presence, her love for Peter and the family, her desire to see Jesus some day. Then He came! Jesus didn't come the way some expected Him to come when the new millennium was ushered in---2000! I think He came in ways we could have missed. In answer to the prayers of millions around the world, wisdom was granted to dedicated people who worked around the clock to find answers to a complicated technology. He has come, moving by his Spirit in nations around the world where revival fires are burning, giving a gift of time to get our homes and nation ready. Perhaps we aren't listening. Jesus comes with strength in times of weakness; He comes with his love to wipe out hate and fear. He comes with wisdom when we ask for it. He comes with trials to strengthen our trust, with fire to purify our faith, like gold. He comes with tenderness to wipe our tears; He knows when we cry in the night. He comes!

Sometimes we miss His coming into our everyday lives because He comes in ways we don't understand. He comes to a broken world, through us, his children, when we learn to listen to His words. I closed Jeanelle's journal, then reached for my five-year planner with the clean white sheets before me. When I turned to the marked-up old planner, filled with notes, dates, airline phone numbers, times, and places, I could only bow in humility and sing the old song: "Great is thy faithfulness, morning and evening, spring, winter, sun, rain, sorrow, joy." You come, Lord Jesus---you were there all the time.

eighteen

The Blow Out

"It won't be long before I'll be home for the summer---that means the beach house, Grammy. Then you can write your stories from the beach chair, and we'll do all the cooking," said Katie Elise. We were on our way to Montreat College in Asheville, North Carolina, where Katie Elise was a freshman. Heading toward Benson on I-40 the car suddenly rattled and shook; Chris calmly maneuvered the nervous car to a safe place off the road. "Oh oh! A blowout, Grammy!" There we sat on the highway and remembered what we forgot---the car phone! Cars kept rolling past, oblivious to the three helpless musketeers on the side of the road. After all, it was Saturday afternoon, and the entire world seemed to be going someplace. Then we hit on an idea! "Katie Elise, sit up on the hood and look helpless." That did it! A handsome young man on his way to NC State stopped to aid the beautiful blonde damsel in distress---then discovered a mother and grandmother in the car. With gracious Southern manners he made the necessary call, and then his car rolled down the road. "I hope you got a picture of me sitting on that hood, Grammy."

An hour later a truck came along to assist us to the repair station where we waited three hours while other cars limped in, wounded and beaten, to the only place open on a Saturday afternoon. A large van managed to slide in before the transmission died; a large family spilled out. "We were on our way to Atlanta to see Grandpa before he died. Now can't get anyone, so maybe we get cars from the airport." With a new tire we were finally on our way, down I-40 to Clemmons Village to see my sister Doris and her husband David, in a beautiful caring facility. I couldn't help but remember that "life is what happens to you while you are making other plans". The blowouts in life come while sailing down the highway of routine---then a rattle and a shake---a stoplight!

The loving atmosphere of Clemmons Village Retirement Home was like a "Welcome Home"---away from home. While Chris visited with David, sitting with his oxygen tank, I took Katie Elise into the adjoining room where my beautiful sister Doris rocked in her contour chair and looked into space. I gathered her in my arms and sobbed, "My sister, my beautiful sister! Oh Doris, how I love you." She looked at me. "I'm Margaret, your sister." "Yes, yes, together---all together---you---you---all together." She laughed and cried and called me "mother". Katie Elise watched with tears in her eyes. "Oh Katie Elise, we were little girls and played together like you and Sarah did; then we grew up together as best friends," I told her. One day a lady watched us five sisters having lunch in a restaurant and asked, "Are you sisters or friends?" Jeanelle answered, "We were born sisters, but chose each other for friends." "Now Grace and Jeanelle are Home with the Lord, Katie Elise. Joyce, Doris and I are left. It goes so fast!"

When Doris says "altogether" I think she remembers something from the past---how we sang around the piano, told stories, swam at the beach, and took long walks around her beautiful home in Stoneville, North Carolina. "The years go too fast, Katie Elise, treasure each day as a gift from God." One time when we five sisters were all together we asked if anyone needed to ask forgiveness for any unkind word or deed. We sat still---shook our heads! No one could think of an unpleasant incident---only love for each other. What a gift! Now the only word Doris seems to remember is "together".

It was time to go. I held Doris in my arms and prayed for God's loving arms to hold her close until He took her Home. When David walked in with Chris, Doris' face lit up with a smile. "Together!" They had been together for more than fifty years. David told Chris about a book he was reading, <u>A Promise Kept</u>, by Dr. R. McQuilkin---a beautiful love story of how Dr. McQuilkin cared for his wife Muriel, who had Alzheimer's. "You need a box of Kleenex, Chris. These wonderful people here tell me I am helping Doris because she feels secure when I am near her." He wiped his eyes. "I brought my organ from home, and I can play for Doris---she likes music. And I have my computer---and all these "angels" for friends." We prayer together, then continued to Montreat to get Katie Elise settled in her dorm room.

I don't know why the blowouts of life come. Perhaps God is telling a love story to a culture consumed with instant gratification---a love story of faithfulness and commitment to God and each other. In this day of searching for power and pleasure, a blowout on the highway of life brings us to a stop. Then we can ponder the greatest truth of all: 'That God so loved the world, He gave His son. ''When the blowouts come, the eternal truth of God's love enables us to continue the journey---Home---all together. We don't live by explanations, Katie Elise; we live by the promises of God. Don't forget to check the Guidebook---the promises are there. You never know when your life might depend on them---even through your freshman year." It was time to say goodbye and head for I-40 to Wilmington. Chris eased out of the driveway with the reminder, "Don't forget to get the picture of Katie Elise on the hood."

nineteen

Full Price

When I pulled out of the driveway I called to Sarah, who was planting flowers in my garden. "While you are at it, Sarah, how about trimming those scraggly front bushes for me?" With a cheerful wave from Sarah, my gardening granddaughter, I was off to the garden center for more plants. Upon my return I was greeted with, "Surprise, Grammy!" In addition to my scraggly bushes, Sarah had managed to manicure my beautiful azalea bushes---just ready to "bust out all over" in time for the Azalea Festival. I took a deep breath. "Thank you!" But I groaned inwardly.

"What happened to your azaleas, Grammy?" Shawn asked on his way to the kitchen to create another omelet. "Sarah gave them a shave and trim. But please don't say anything---she thought it was a surprise." It was! "But she'll be devastated when she finds out, because she enjoys gardens." "I know! I'll find the right time to tell her so she'll know for the future. No one works harder than Sarah---good grades in college, and then helps me clean the house and garden. I'd rather have scalped azaleas than a wounded Sarah." "Okay," he agreed, "I won't say anything, but it looks weird."

In the trunk of my car I had a bag of fertilizer, red potatoes, Kentucky wonder bush beans, squash, Swiss chard and cucumber seeds, six "Better Boy" tomato plants and six green pepper plants, all set to plant in the freshly tilled garden, but it would have to wait. I had a story to write, so with pen in hand I retreated to my office and wrote a short story for children called "High Button Shoes". "Oh me," I sighed when I remembered that I was to write another Sparkle (tiny angel) story for Easter. Spring somehow slipped into my office and took me by the hand, and I followed the sunshine trail with my hoe and shovel. When Sarah pulled into the driveway after class she too followed the call of spring and we decided the stories could wait, the garden couldn't. While Sarah dug the holes, I popped the cut potatoes into the prepared places and covered the holes with my foot.

"Look, Grammy! That black cloud---whoops, here it comes!" With buckets and shovels we ran, but it was too late. We were drenched in the flash rain storm. Laughing and dripping, we managed to get showers and into dry clothes. "Wow that was sudden!" "Oh look! The sun is out. Come on, let's finish the garden." I was dry and clean---not too anxious to get all muddy again---but I had good help, so we headed out to the potato patch and planted the onions, beans, tomatoes, and squash. "We can plant the rest later. But look---it's coming again!" The sky opened and sheets of rain drenched us again---but we had finished and ran to the house.

"This time, I'm not going out again---three times and you're out! Let's go to Wal-Mart for a good hot dog, then to the garden shop for plants for your daddy's shop." With a trunk full of plants for Ralph's shop, The Master's Touch, we stopped at Cloth World to see the new spring material. Sarah lost herself in the rows of endless bolts of colorful spring fabric, then stopped in the designer section and held a bolt of beautiful gray material with a border of pink embroidery. "It's not on sale," she said. Then we moved to other material, half price, and found a lovely blue fabric and another material with butterflies. "Oh, this is great for summer." We placed the blue and butterfly material in the basket, but I watched Sarah return to look at the gray and pink designer cloth---then walk away.

It was then I remembered what my sister Jeanelle told me about her Jewish friend, Sid, "Look, Sid---this was 50% of, and this was 75% off. What a bargain!" "Very good, very good---a good shopper you are---good taste, but my friend, let me tell you something; once in a while pay full price---good for the soul." When we rang up the lovely cloth, half price, I reached for the designer fabric---$23.00 a yard---and paid full price. Sarah was Papa's princess, and I could almost hear him say, "Good---full price. She's worth it!"

The next week we headed to Gloria, the seamstress, who would enjoy sewing for "my Sarah" and could appreciate half price, but also full price!

When evening came the doors were shut, shades drawn, and I curled up in Harold's chair. It had been a good day. A fence around the garden kept Scarlet from digging up the potatoes; a gentle rain washed the plants. With Scarlet's head in my lap I opened up my book, America's Real War, by Rabbi Daniel Lapin, and realized how great Americans have paid full price for us to live in freedom. "Our nation is in an internal war between those who seek a secular future and those who call for a return to America's Judeo-Christian roots." I pondered long about the principles of honor---God, family, and society around us; that in my youth the biblical principles, not theology, held school, church, and home together. The author continued, "A weakened Christianity in America threatens all Americans, including Jews."

Our parents and grandparents came to America and paid the price in toil, sweat, and tears to give the next generation the blessings of a free people to live out biblical principles in our communities. Corrie ten Boom's family paid "full price" for their defense of the Jews; our Norwegian and Danish grandparents hid the Jews in caves or fishing boats. It was the belief in biblical principles that enabled statesmen like Wilberforce to stand against slavery. What price will America pay for the unheard cries of the unborn that are on the bargain table---*choice!*

In the Old Testament God says to choose life---or death. Of course we should desire life, but the price is obedience to God's rules. Psalm 1 gives a picture of choices. If obedience to God's rules is difficult, the choice to disobey has even more devastating consequences. As a nation we can choose to live by the Judeo-Christian principles, not theology, or we can choose a secular road with no absolutes. Consequences follow.

Jesus said, "I am the way, the truth, and the life." The cross stands, not affected by the winds of changing culture; choose life with God. "Beneath the cross of Jesus I take my stand." The cries of life will reveal our choices in the alone hours. Jesus, alone, prayed, "Not my will, but thine be done." To the sleeping disciples he said, "Come, let us be going." The battle has been won! On the cross, Jesus cried, "It is finished!' The price is paid---full price!

twenty

The Clipped Azaleas

The azaleas were bustin' out all over town---white, pink, peach, red and purple competing for attention. Dilapidated buildings hid behind the colorful display that continued to grow and bloom in spite of neglect. When I looked out of my breakfast room I saw the plum trees in red competing with the stately pear trees in solid white. Each year I planted small azaleas to fill the lonely places in my garden; today the small plants were in full color.

When Sarah came through the gate she called out, "Wow! Grammy, look at those colorful plants. But what happened to the big ones?" Reluctantly I showed her how she had clipped the wrong bushes---just ready to bloom. "Oh no, I didn't realize they were azaleas---and I guess I did surprise you."

"Pruning won't hurt those plants, and just wait until next year---they will outshine the entire garden. Now we have Mexican heather, verbena, phlox, and yellow day lilies to plant. If we plant enough perennials we can serve eviction notices to the weeds---less to plant next year. That's what I said last year, but I keep planting more every year. What I need now are some hanging baskets and the bird feeders refilled. Always enough work to do outside, so when it rains, we can clean the house. My problem is that I should be writing. So, I guess you will clean the house so I can hide in my office."

Instead of doing either we just took off to Wal-Mart for a hog dog (getting to be a habit), then to pick up hanging plants that read "Swedish Ivy". Well now, that caught my attention, and I decided Swedish Ivy went along with Norwegian coffee and Danish pastry. My grandson Chad used to say that our house was a summer house. "What's a summer house, Chad?" "Oh, it's a fun place--even in the winter---so that makes it a summer house all year.'

I like that! A summer house! Now we are getting ready for the big beach house where the ocean breezes blow, the seagulls cry, and the waves wash up on the shore. Sarah and I were determined to get these gardens in good shape, with pine straw and bark and low white fences to keep Scarlet out. After all, Shawn was graduating in May, and his friends from Gordon College were coming to the land of azaleas and dogwoods. I had to admit that the "crew cut" azaleas looked rather lonely, surrounded by living color.

It was time for Sarah to return to classes and study---a time to put hoes and shovels in the garden shed and call it a day. When evening came I found myself in the big chair---the Papa chair---then I drew a notebook from the lower shelf: Biblical Studies---Harold E. Jensen. I leafed through the yellow pages of meticulous, handwritten notes from seminary days. Every page was clearly outlined in flawless script; the returned tests were graded from 90 to 100. I kept turning the pages through blurred vision and wondered why I hadn't noticed his mind thirsting for knowledge; I only saw the heart devoted to God. Was I so occupied with the so-called "Lord's work" that I didn't understand that we are all in the Lord's work---science, the arts, sociology, theology, etc. ---that what we believe will be lived out in the market place? Was my Harold an "azalea bush", clipped too soon before he completed his studies at Loyola University---on his way to a doctorate degree? Did the tyranny of the urgent eclipse the dream?

I leafed through notes that read that the function of knowledge was to grow and develop, to solve problems, adjust to environment, to construct thoughts and ideas. In the notes I caught a line from Shakespeare: "The web of our life is mingled yarn, good and ill". Then I wondered if we had somehow missed the tide at the molten moment. "There is a tide in the affairs of men when taken at the flood, moves on to fortune." (Shakespeare) I found myself weeping. "Oh Lord, what if we miss the "flood" and find ourselves in the "shallows"?

It was then I remembered Mama's yarn basket---mingled yarn of all colors, bits and pieces left over from the skeins of yarn. Quietly she rocked and knitted the mingled yarn of all colors into a colorful afghan. Then she put the empty basket away and folded her hands in thanksgiving to God. Nothing was wasted. "So God wastes nothing, Margaret; for out of the mingled yarn of life He works together for good," my Mama said.

I reached for my father's Bible with the yellowed sermon notes. "The Bible should be our mentor, monitor, and our memento more; our remembrance and keeper of our conscience." (Spurgeon) In one of my father's rare wistful moments he confided to me that his secret dream was to get his doctor's degree in theology from a great university, but he had been persuaded to minister to the new immigrants. The dream was buried, but he remained faithful to God and his people. But was my father another "azalea bush" clipped too soon? "Man comes to a sense of his own greatness, only after he humbles himself before the majesty of God," my Papa said. If we miss the tide's flow, do we live in despair in the shallows? Within the yellow pages I read answers to probably his own questions.

It read, "God does not want us to cringe in fear and despair. God wants us to stand up---a new creation in Christ---to stand tall, erect, *and ready to obey.* There can be no pride when we realize that we are bought with a price: *'For God so loved the world that He gave his only begotten son that whosoever believeth in him should not perish but have everlasting live.'"* (John 3:16) He died for all of us who missed the molten moments, whose dreams went out with the tide, who found ourselves in the shallows of defeat and despair.

That is when Jesus comes, reaching for us. "Come, all you who are weary and heavy laden. Come, come---together we walk and talk and learn of me." What an invitation! God offers grace, mercy, forgiveness, and a new beginning. Through the years we learn that the "dark threads are as needful in the weaver's skillful hands as the threads of gold and silver in the pattern he has planned." (Streams in the Desert) Softly the night seemed to fold up another day in a blanket---time to turn out the lights. Scarlet was asleep on her pillow. Life was simple: a bowl of food, water, and a pat---"good girl"---makes her life complete. The grandfather clock struck midnight before I put the notebook and Bible on the shelf. One day someone asked my father why he preached so often on grace and mercy. "Oh ja, grace and mercy is what I know best." To myself I thought, "Matchless grace of Jesus, mighty as the rolling ocean, big enough to take care of life's tides, ebb, and flow." I turned out the light.

twenty–one

No Soy Sauce on Ice Cream

At the conclusion of the benediction at Myrtle Grove Presbyterian Church I eased through the crowd to the parking lot
when Ralph tapped me on the shoulder. 'Mom, I'm bringing
a new couple home for Sunday dinner. See you at the house."
With a wave that said 'okay' I hurried to my car to get home
first---to boil water for the corn. Chris would follow and put
two more settings on the table and fill the glasses with ice. We
were a team to get dinner on the table, and when I was out of
town Chris had Sunday dinner. I reached for the soy sauce,
since I had changed the menu to chop suey and rice---but I
don't think I'll do that again. Roast beef, mashed potatoes,
and apple pie seem better suited for Sunday. Within a short
time Ralph came with our new friends, Caroline and Gary, and
we were blended together around the table where conversation
flowed freely about the great biblical sermons preached by our
Pastor, Stephen Crotts.

When Ralph reached for the soy sauce he said, "Mom, this
reminds me of when we took in eleven Vietnamese for four
months---you must tell the story." Since I grew up in a pastor's
home that was open to Norwegian immigrants, I just carried
that tradition into our generation. Before we had the Vietnam-

ese we had "hippies". Oh, yes, we did. After Ralph returned from the "far country" (oh yes, he was my "hippie rebel") his friends decided to come and see what changed Ralph. During 1971 we had about seventy hippies; not all at once, but we had nineteen one weekend---six from one family. Two lived with us for six months. Today Kevin is a dedicated missionary in Mexico, and Jeremy and Jesse; his two fine sons are graduates of Gordon College!

It all began July 1975 when the plane, on its last lap of the journey from Asia, slipped out from behind the clouds and made a gentle landing at the Greensboro Airport. Stan and Ginny Smith, missionaries from Vietnam, watched with us as Pastor An, a Vietnamese pastor, and his family stepped out of the plane. Their two teenage boys were swallowed up in Navy coats, and the mother held her daughters closely as they came toward us. I was touched by their weariness, their gaunt expressions. When they saw the Smiths though, hope rose in their faces and their eyes brightened. A tearful reunion made us realize how dear these people were to the missionaries--- and how much all had suffered. As a family we had watched the tragic news of the fall of Vietnam and our son Dan had wondered about the fate of the veteran missionaries, Gordon and Laura Smith. "I wonder if they made it to safety," Dan had said. "I'll never forget their visit with me in the Da Nang Hospital." Just before being shipped out Dan had a severe kidney infection. He later learned that most of his company had died in battle. A phone call to the United World Mission reassured us that the senior Smiths were safe at home. Their concern was for their son Stan and his wife Ginny. Stan and Ginny were among the last to leave Saigon. Then came the pleas, "We need sponsors for two Vietnamese pastors now in USA camps."

So a council meeting of the Jensens around the dining room table resulted in our sponsoring the two families of Pastor An and Pastor Dicht---eleven Vietnamese who spoke no English. Pastor Dicht and his family arrived later. In the meantime, Chris, Ralph, and two-year-old Shawn, who were waiting to get into their new home, were temporarily housed with us. Into this setting Eric was born---to the delight of the Vietnamese, who love children deeply.

I had been taught well by my Norwegian mama to take one day at a time---more often, one hour at a time. Mama's home had been filled with Norwegian immigrants---but she shared their language and culture. We Jensens had another language and a different culture from these Vietnamese families. Chris set up classes for English lessons. Harold found work for the men, and the women were introduced to American housekeeping. Vietnamese words and English words posted on the refrigerator kept up the limited communications. The children knew no barriers, and they played easily together.

Pastor Roy Putnam of Trinity Church not only opened his heart, but he also opened the doors of the church for Christian fellowship. The response of this wonderful church provided housing for the Vietnamese missionaries; it also provided love and understanding to help bind up the wounds of broken dreams. Everything had been left behind, including the two ministers' churches, Bible schools, and orphanages. Gordon and Laura Smith had done extensive work establishing those orphanages, as well as Bible schools and churches, and a renowned medical center and clinic for lepers. Gordon Smith was determined to return! He especially wanted to take tapes, and other help, to the blind. He was sure the Viet Cong would recognize his lifetime of service to the people of Vietnam and allow him to return. The younger missionary, Stan Smith, knew better. Horror stories followed, not only in the news but also in firsthand reports from these faithful Vietnamese pastors. Pastor An had been able to rescue more than twenty orphans in his jeep and move them through the precarious jungle. When they came to an impassable river where bridges had been destroyed, Pastor An cried out to God, "You delivered Moses; make a way for us." An Army helicopter appeared, rescued them, and took them all to Saigon. From Saigon they were airlifted to America.

Mrs. An grieved for her three youngest children, left behind with their grandparents when the communists blocked the roads. Pastor An had rescued the orphans, but he could not rescue his own. His grief was deep. The work and dreams of a lifetime seemed to crumble under the tyranny of the ruthless enemy. Churches, orphanages, clinics, and schools were all destroyed. What a waste! The missionaries and the faithful pastors believed that out of the ashes of ruin God would raise up a people of faith---and He did! The Dicht family fled the Viet Cong and managed to find safety on an enormous barge along with hundreds of others---only to be shot at by the soldiers on the shore. The ropes were cut and the overcrowded barge drifted out to sea without food or water. Pastor Dicht was left for dead among the baggage. His wife and daughter prayed! Rain came and washed over the lifeless form of the father and when he moved the wife called, "He's alive! Don't throw him overboard." Then an American ship rescued them.

Bit by bit we heard the stories and marveled at how these people had survived. Now they had to learn a new language and adjust to a foreign culture. A cynical reporter asked me, "How do you expect to feed all these people?" "Oh," I laughed, "don't you know the story of the fish and the loaves in the Bible?" He didn't! When I came home, someone had brought cans of tuna fish, and the Pillsbury Company had sent cases of bread mixes. Talk about the loaves and fishes! I thought the story too good to miss, so I wrote to the president of Pillsbury to let him know his company was part of a miracle. He was delighted! Everyone likes to be part of a miracle. We saw miracles every day.

One day a hundred pound bag of rice was on the porch, along with a gallon of soy sauce. Our guests put soy sauce on everything---toast, eggs, rice, etc. One day we made home-made ice cream and I announced, "No soy sauce on ice cream! American tradition!" That settled it. Trips to the mall were hilarious, especially when the dignified men bowed to the mannequins and said, "Good morning."

Dr. James Bruce gave free physicals. English classes were offered, along with tutoring services. Businessmen from Trinity Church offered work. We kept a shuttle service going: doctor, English classes, work, and church. Janice, our daughter, flew down from Boston to help with household chores, and she offered some good advice. "Let the women cook." They were elated! They caught fish in the lake (no one else caught fish), and they cleaned the fish in our driveway. The hose was handy. They sat on the floor and slivered string beans or cut a chicken up in small pieces so fast I couldn't keep up with them. I watched them stir-fry one of those cut up chickens, then add vegetables, and finally put that delicious concoction around a mountain of rice. They must have choked on my mashed potatoes, meat balls, and creamed vegetables---Norskie style.

In the meantime, Dan and Gordon and Laura Smith drew up plans for mobile homes on Shalom Farm. Harold purchased three mobile homes with air conditioning and our dreams soared. This would be a temporary transition period for them--time to learn the language and culture, a chance to grow their own gardens and raise chickens.

But our dreams again were changed. After the two families had been in our home four months, someone made lovely downtown apartments available to them. Their adjustment to city life was amazing. We had underestimated their ability to adapt to their new world. The mobile homes were sold. God had a better plan.

Within a short time Laura and Gordon Smith went home to be with the Lord. How the courts of heaven must have resounded with, "Welcome home, good and faithful servants."

After years of prayer and working through various organizations---and by means of negotiations and money---the Ans were reunited with the three children they were forced to leave behind in Vietnam. When we were informed of the reunion, we saw it as a miracle. The news media had pictures of Pastor An tearfully embracing his children, teenagers by that time. The Dicht family is pastoring in California. Our cultural exchange was a comedy of errors---and most of the errors were mine. One day, though, Harold---upset about some political deal reported in the morning paper---pounded his fist on the breakfast table. The Vietnamese immediately went into a huddle! Often, when they didn't understand something, they went into a huddle.

Poor Stan had to interpret all these huddles to us. About the fist-banging, the Vietnamese concluded, "Jensens are in big fight!" Poor Harold! He had to read the newspaper---and smile---whether he liked what he was reading or not! Another huddle and another interpretation. I had asked Harold to take out the garbage can on his way to the car. "Poor Mr. Jensen has to do woman's work," the pastors said. Harold loved it! Finally I said, "Okay, when I go to Vietnam, I'll do it the Vietnamese way. In America we all help! American tradition!" That did it! Harold took out the garbage.

I'm a hugger---and made the mistake of hugging everyone! It took much interpretation for the men! The priceless moments were when we read the scriptures, prayed, and sang together. The bond of Christian love transcends all barriers. The first Christmas together was a moving experience. My Norwegian mama gave a reading while Stan interpreted. Pastor An read the Christmas story in Vietnamese, and they sang their carols. We did the same in English. (God understands both!)

Many changes have come since 1975. The Vietnamese joined with us when our brother Gordon was buried in the family plot on the Hammer home place, beside my Norwegian Papa. They understood. They had lived with death, but they also knew that "Jesus is the resurrection and the life". Someday we would all be together again. They loved our Norwegian Mama because they have great respect for the wisdom that comes with age. And she understood their struggles. She told stories about coming to America herself and about learning English and adapting to new customs. There was no barrier in love. They heard her with their hearts.

At Christmas time in 1989 we received a beautiful letter from Hoi (Henry), the eldest son of Pastor An. He wrote:

> *I've been married for six months now and love every minute of it. I'm serving as a pastor of a Vietnamese Baptist Church in Tacoma, Washington. Besides that I am also attending the Golden Gate Baptist Theological Seminary on the Northwest Campus in Portland, Oregon. I have never been so sure in my life that this is what God wants me to do, and I know He can use me---although sometimes I wonder why---to do his work.*

Love in Christ
Henry Hoi Phan

They all made it in the new land. God is faithful!

It was 4 p.m. and we were still sitting at the dinner table. That's how it was in my family, listening to stories from far away places. Then many years later I penned them on yellow pads. Some of our happiest moments in life come from sharing around a dinner table---almost a lost art in our fast food culture. The day came to an end when we reluctantly said goodbye to our "adopted" friends---but with a reminder that the door is always open.

twenty–two

The New Growth

I pulled up the blinds to let the morning sun fill the breakfast room while the coffee pot perked a happy tune. When the cinnamon toast popped up, I sat down with my coffee mug and buttered toast and thanked God for a new day. To think I didn't want to come here twenty-five years ago, and now I love every corner of this house, my beautiful office, and the gardens around me.

I came with a heavy heart to leave the familiar. My steps were slow---*but I came*---out of obedience to God and respect for Harold's decision. Looking back, it was the best move we ever made, but I didn't come leaping and praising God. I came with one step in front of the other, but in the right direction---obedience to God. When I turned the pages of My Utmost For His Highest, by Oswald Chambers, I read a passage I had marked many years ago:

> *If I obey Jesus Christ in the haphazard circumstances, they become pinholes through which we see the face of God and when we stand face to face with God, I will discover thousands were blessed.*

About the time I was feeling "spiritual" I heard the Jeep in the driveway. "Stopped by to give you a hug, Grammy---and make an omelet before I run to class." Shawn, with a cap on backwards and my old apron to protect his jeans, fried onions to compete with cinnamon toast. With a "clean up your mess" I was out the back door to look over the garden. It was then I noticed new green leaves on the clipped azalea bushes. From my office in back of the garage I called Jan. Believe me, we keep the telephone economy booming.

I remember when Harold would wave the telephone bill in front of me when I was talking to our daughter and ask, "Are you interested in this!" "Oh no," I answered, "I don't like details, just general ideas. Besides, I don't drink, don't smoke, and I do my own hair." That did it! He always lost on that one and told Jan, "I'm in a no-win situation."

One morning when Jan called she asked, "What is my dear Daddy doing?" "Oh, he's making our bed, I answered. "I thought he only made his side of the king size bed," said Jan. "This morning *I'm still in it!*" Jan couldn't stop laughing. By the time Jan answered the phone I was laughing at the memories---then she joined me. What an incredible gift---memories! "What are you doing, Mom?" Jan asked. "I just escaped to my office while the master chef is at it again---his famous omelet." You'll never die from boredom, Mom." "By the way Jan---I just spotted some new shoots on the clipped azaleas. Gives me hope for the future. For several days I have been going through my father's sermon notes and I found myself in tears over what seemed to be missed opportunities. Do you have time to hear some of the notes?" I asked. "I'll get my coffee cup and listen." "This note got me when my father wrote, 'How do you go on when no one is listening?' He answered, 'Life is a campaign, not a holiday.' Another question: 'Why am I sent to work where circumstances are adverse?' He answered, 'We go on to tell the story of God's love for mankind.' Another question: 'Am I merely a man exposed to pain, conflict, and failure?' He answered, 'It is in the battle where we prove our mettle.'

"Oh, Jan, I wish I could have known him---a lonely orphan who probably held a deep loneliness in his soul; a loneliness that God's love filled---and Mama's unconditional love. No wonder God warns us not to judge; we never know the depth of need in another person." Jan replied, "Bestefar and Bestemor's (grandpa and grandma's) dreams didn't die. They weren't azalea bushes clipped too soon, but new shoots were sent into seven children who love God. And their children are blessed and a blessing."

When we get to the beach house, Mom, bring the notes and let us give the new generation a glimpse of the faith of their fathers, living still, in spite of broken dreams. That will bring strength to the young green leaves in new branches." Then Jan hung up, off to tend to her dinner for 50 tonight.

I looked at the bushes in front of my office door---young green leaves glistening in the sun---and remembered my Norwegian Mama. It was Jan's beloved Bestemor who served soup and whole wheat bread to the lonely immigrants while her Bestefar played the guitar and told stories of faith. Today the gracious first lady of Gordon College was setting a beautiful table with her flower arrangements, working with a capable food service team---but it is Jan's joyous welcome that makes the guests feel they are in a warm summer house, even in New England winters. My Norwegian Mama, with a bowl of violets on a starched table cloth, served the oatmeal or soup with the flair of a gracious hostess.

From the notebook and sermon notes I read again of the love for God's Word. Then I opened the book written by Jan, The Hungry Heart, a devotional from the Old Testament. "Another generation grew up who knew not the Lord, nor what He had done for Israel." (Judges 2:10) "Handing down faith from one generation to the next is God's pattern for relaying truth: now a new generation plucked grapes they had not planted, drew water from wells they had not dug---choice by choice, tiny but tangible gods replaced the God of their fathers. A fresh generation stood knee deep in grapes, but empty of gratitude. They forgot their deliverer." I stopped to thank God for the branch---green with life. "When God's redemption comes to the point of obedience, it always creates. The redemption of God will rush through us to other lives. Behind the deed of obedience is the reality of Almighty God." (Oswald Champers)

The beach chair waits for the stories to be written...Sarah's clipped azaleas, Shawn's burnt onions, pilgrims from Vietnam, hippies, and God's grace.

twenty–three

For Everything A Season

I eased my bags through the rusty gate and moved cautiously through the path between overgrown vines and orange day lilies. Then I climbed the wooden steps where I dropped my bags on the long wooden table on the screened porch. The hammock looked inviting, but that was for the young; the rocking chair was for me. I was alone! It didn't seem possible that a year had passed, and the family was on their way again to the beach house. I chuckled to myself, remembering how Chad had thrown out his arms to the ocean and wind. "I love it! I love it! It's like we've been here forever!"

For a year I had been writing in my notebook: hurricanes, floods, blizzards, and blowouts. Now Chris and Jan were at the fish market to buy fresh shrimp for supper. In a few hours we would gather around the picnic table to enjoy the shrimp and corn on the cob while watching the sun splash the last colors of the day over the sound. I leaned back and rocked while I remembered February, when I was in Sarasota Baptist Church to speak at a women's luncheon...

A phone call came from Ralph, "Uncle Howard has gone Home, Mama!" My host, Bob Hoffman, checked flights. Then

I was on my way to Little Rock, Arkansas, where family and friends gathered in a memorial tribute to Howard Jensen, beloved husband of fifty-three years to my sister Joyce, devoted father to Judy, Paul, and Steve, and loving brother of my Harold. Not only was Howard the dearest grandfather to his eight grandchildren, but the best uncle in the world to our children. Now the three brothers---Jack, Harold, and Howard---were Home! Joyce and I were left to pray for the children; not only our children, but also brother Gordon's. Mother and Dad had prayed for all of us; then Uncle Jack called out the names of all the family; now Joyce and I were left to continue to pray that each new generation will walk in obedience to God. Before our tears were dry we received another message---sister Doris' husband of more than fifty years had died in his sleep. Once again we stood beside an open grave while Jeanelle's son, Dr. Robert Keiter, read "Let not your hearts be troubled." "Dust to dust, ashes to ashes. David Hammer's soul has winged its way Home." Rob's beautiful voice sang over the valley and mountains, "Because He lives I can face tomorrow." The beautiful home overlooking the valley and mountains is silent, and the wind blows over the graves of Mother, Dad, Gordon, Alice, Grace, Jeanelle, and David Hammer. While Doris slept in her own peaceful world, the family and friends gathered together to bring strength and comfort to each other. God's comforting love fills the empty places in the heart.

I rocked while seagulls cried and the hammock swayed in the summer breeze. Sorrows make places in the heart for joy---enough room for the joy of two new beautiful baby girls, Lily and Gracynne, my great granddaughters. For everything there is a season---a time to mourn and a time to rejoice. Now was the time for joy! I checked play pens, high chairs, and strollers---even gates---for safety.

When I heard car doors slam I knew Chris and Jan had returned with shrimp and corn. Shawn was sent to get ice for the ice cream freezer. The others headed to the beach for a swim. Since I had been ordered out of the kitchen last year I knew better than to invade that sacred domain, so I headed back to the beach chair with two beautiful babies on my lap. We rocked and sang and watched the seagulls over the ocean waves. Lily couldn't wait to climb the stairs, while Gracynne checked out the lay of the land to be sure Eric, her daddy, was in view. Watching the new grandfathers, Jud and Ralph, got higher ratings than any movie.

When the call came, "Dinner is ready," there was a scramble for t-shirts over damp bathing suits, jostling for places on benches and chairs, then quiet when hands joined in prayer for a blessing over the food and family. The conversation erupted about everyone's activities. Eric did it again---slid the corn over the butter dish. The babied banged spoons, delighting in the attention from aunts and uncles, grandparents, and even their *great* Grammy. (Respect, if you don't mind.) Sarah's version is, "I love it, I love it---everybody talking at the same time and no one listening." Chad couldn't stop taking movies and recording stories, at the same time describing the documentary he was filming about baseball in the Dominican Republic. Shawn took a few bows when we congratulated him on graduating from Cameron School of Business, University of North Carolina at Wilmington. While Heather took a year off to care for Lily, Matt received his masters of Public Health from Harvard. Next month Heather and Mat will return to Temple University to complete their final year in medical school. Katie Elise told about her great year at Montreat. Sarah told stories about her summer job, between college classes. Somehow life goes on---funerals, births, weddings, family reunions. For everything---there is a season.

A beautiful wedding in Atlanta brought the truth of the value of friendship. Shawn was asked to be an attendant at Terry Redmile's (his high school friend) wedding. It just happened to be during our beach week. Joan and Jeff Redmile, dear friends, had been in Spain for five years, and then returned to Texas. We kept in touch through notes and letters. "Ralph, how can we leave when everyone is coming to the beach?" I commented. "The question is, Mother, how can we *not* go---our friends are home from Spain, and it is time to renew our friendship." So it came to pass that Shawn and Katie Elise drove; Ralph, Chris, and I flew Delta and arrived in the same hotel with the Redmiles. We couldn't stop talking---Terry, Brandy (the daughter), Joan and Jeff; like Sara would say "everybody talking at once---no one listening". Only we *were* listening. We heard the loneliness of a strange place, new language, returning home where family and friends had moved. We also heard how we had been so involved in all our family struggles that we didn't move over and give time and space for friends. In all the glamour of Stephanie and Terry's beautiful wedding---the festivities at the country club, meeting new people---the true joy was the cultivation of old friends. Even in a large family like ours we must make room for friends. For everything---there is a season, a time for family and a time for friends.

twenty–four

Faith Lights

It was time to close the beach house. High chairs, strollers, and play pens were stored for another day. Tanned by the sun and sea the beachers eased their packed cars out of the driveway and turned to the roads leading north, south, east, and west. "We'll be back," echoed in the wind. I rocked alone in my beach chair. Memories came on slippered feet to take a stage bow before the curtain came down on another day of the drama of life. Years turn into golden moments when joy and sorrow, laughter and tears weave a strange pattern of the tapestry of time.

"The dark threads are as needful
In the Master's skillful hand
As the threads of gold and silver
In the pattern He has planned."   Streams in The Desert

Where had all the years of watching the ever-changing ocean gone? It seemed like yesterday when Jan ran out on the pier to sit beside Grandpa Jensen, dressed in his long underwear. "Grandpa, you are in your B.V.D.'s!" With a deep chuckle he added, "I'm more covered than you are." They sat together, his white hair glistening in the sun, Jan's blonde head on his shoulder. Grandma Jensen was frying flounder for supper---in butter; no margarine for the Danish cook. The Norwegian grandma Tweten, was sitting on a blanket telling stories to Chad and Heather, curled up in her lap. Now Heather tells stories to her daughter Lily. Now Mama and Papa, they are gone! Joyce and I are left of this generation, while Doris, in her own world, waits to go Home to join the others. We rock while our children take over the plans. One day, when wondering about the younger ones, Shawn (the King of the Omelets) said, "Oh Grammy, you know how close Chad and I are. We will always keep the families together." "Lord, increase my faith!" When I wrapped my sweater around me I was reminded that with autumn's falling leaves there comes a whisper of a winter wind. I could almost hear my Norwegian mama say, "Oh ja, when winter comes, then remember the next thing to come is spring---and the bluebirds."

A plane flying overhead reminded me of the day Jan and I had to catch a shuttle from Oregon to Seattle, then to the east coast. It was 4:30 AM. We dragged our bags into the dreary airport. In a corner of the airport a man had set up a small kitchen to serve the early travelers breakfast while they were waiting for the often delayed shuttle flights. "What a great idea" was the comment by travelers as we used paper plates and cups to hold crisp bacon, scrambled eggs, coffee, and toast. The dreary airport became alive with happy campers enjoying a quick breakfast together. Then we were on our way---a long journey to Boston for Jan; Wilmington, North Carolina, for me. When I flew over my city late at night, I saw the welcome lights of home.

For a moment I wondered what God sees when He scans the earth. I recalled a passage of scripture that says the trial of our faith is more precious than gold. Without faith it is impossible to please God. Just as lights welcomed me home to Wilmington, does God see 'faith' as lights in a dark world?" I read where the life of faith is not mounting up with wings, but walking and not fainting; that God engineers the circumstances so we are brought to a place where faith is worked out in actualities. Faith is tested through conflict. Did God see our fathers coming by faith from Europe to a new world as "faith lights" to the next generation? Their hopes and dreams didn't die but lit the way for a new generation. The "lights" live on in music, drama, art, creative writing, administrative skills, teaching, judiciary, medicine, business, theology, etc.---all light in a dark world; "full time Christian service" with a biblical world view in our secular culture. The stories of yesterday rekindle "faith lights" for tomorrow. I see the lights of Home, and I pray that God sees us as "faith lights" in a dark world.

For a moment I closed my eyes and thought of families around the world, coming together around camp fires, rivers, mountains---even second floor flats in throbbing cities like Chicago. Then I wept at the reunion of North and South Koreans that brought children and parents together to mourn the lost years and to rejoice in hope for the next generation. "Faith lights" illuminate the darkness for those who come behind us. Faith is the grasping of almighty power, the hand of man on the arm of God; the grand and blessed hour in which things impossible to me become possible.

It was time to close my memory journal and turn the beach chair to the wall. Then I eased my way between the overgrown vines and closed the rusty gate. The car moved slowly over the bridge toward home. It was time for a cup of tea, so I turned on the television to catch the news---but somehow flipped over to the end of a rerun of the Waltons. For a moment I was caught up in the Waltons heading for the mountains to plant flowers on Grandpa Walton's grave. Grandma Walton's "you old fool", said with tears, was the language of love. Ben promised to take care of Grandpa's tools; each one had a plant and memory. Then Mary Ellen held up the baby with a promise to tell the story of Walton's mountain. Jason reached for the harmonica and played an old hymn, while the family returned to the old house where lights went out to "goodnight".

We may not have had a Walton's mountain, but thank you, Harold, for you knew the ocean would call us all together. Perhaps the next generation will find a mountain, but as for me, I'll stay here. It was time to put Scarlet in the laundry room, turn out the lights, and draw the shades on another day. Tomorrow I'll call Joyce and tell her I closed the journal. We'll pray that those who come behind us find us as "faith lights".

PS: Tomorrow I'll get another notebook---no telling what this new year holds. If I don't write it down though, I'll forget.